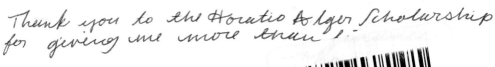

Thank you to the Horatio Adger Scholarship
for giving me more than I...

D0437417

GO, AND DO THE SAME

SCHOOLING A NEW GENERATION FOR HAITI

——————— RODRIGUE MORTEL, M.D. ———————

CATHEDRAL
FOUNDATION PRESS

PUBLISHED BY

CATHEDRAL
FOUNDATION PRESS
© 2018, RODRIGUE MORTEL, M.D.
www.HighHopesForHaiti.org

Printed and bound in the United States of America
First Edition 1 2 3 4 5
Library of Congress Catalog Card Number 2018014717
ISBN 978-1885938541

PUBLISHED BY: Cathedral Foundation Press
PUBLISHER: Christopher Gunty
COVER AND BOOK DESIGN: Sara Travlos
PHOTOS: All photos courtesy Rodrigue Mortel
PRINTED IN THE USA

This book is dedicated
To the *poorest* and *forgotten*
children of Haiti.

CONTENTS

FOREWORDS

As a Catholic living in the Archdiocese of Baltimore since 1989, I had read about Rodrigue Mortel from time to time in the archdiocesan newspaper, The Catholic Review, mostly about the schools he started in Haiti and other projects within his purview as director of the Office of Missions.

He and his work came closer when my parish paired with another in the Diocese of Gonaïves, Haiti for an exchange of faith, culture and support. Fellow parishioners returned from trips there brimming with joy and commitment to the sister relationship formed between the two churches. Next I found myself volunteering for the annual Haiti Carnival festival that brings my parish together for an evening of celebration, fun and fellowship, and devotes the resulting proceeds to our sister parish. Finally, I was asked to assist in writing this book.

None of these remote connections quite prepared me for my encounter of the man himself. In our first meeting, he welcomed me as a partner in his work, making it feel as if I were being welcomed into his home. Dr. Mortel's hope for his motherland of Haiti is infectious, as are his confidence and enthusiasm for realizing that hope in concrete results.

Enjoy the jovial manner, the mischievous smile, the regaling with amusing stories, but do not be fooled. Dr. Mortel is dead serious about accomplishing his vision: bringing forth a new generation of Haitians through a model of better, more accessible education, most especially for the poorest among them. The vision came to him not as a mid-life crisis but as an epiphany that occurred near the beginning of what turned out to be a long, highly successful career in medicine. Even as advancement and new opportunities came rapidly in medicine—and with them, honors and recognition within and beyond the profession—the calling to serve this new vision kept growing within him. Dr. Mortel's retirement from the Penn State College of Medicine in 2001 was simply a switch from part-time to full-time service in his new calling to bring better education to Haiti.

As recounted in this book, the schools he has started in St. Marc, where he grew up, are making major headway. The model works. Now Dr. Mortel is looking for imitators, for others who will take this model and replicate it elsewhere in the country.

He makes it look easy. Don't be fooled by that, either. The partnerships Dr. Mortel has built among church and other charitable organizations took years of cultivation, persistence and talent. One secret of his success is the knack for attracting curious friends and colleagues to accompany him on his frequent trips to the schools in St. Marc to see for themselves what is happening there. Most come back, as he puts it, "with a love of Haiti in their hearts," and often a willingness to commit to support of the work.

Dr. Mortel is confident there are others who will feel called as he was to form their own coalitions of support for schools that lift up the poor of Haiti. He shows here how it can be done, and the abundant blessings that follow.

Read this book and you may find yourself asking Dr. Mortel for an invitation to visit. Maybe you will be the next one to take the lead in building up education in other parts of the country. It all starts with that love of Haiti in the heart.

Jay G. Merwin, Jr.
Baltimore, 2018

Hopefully many will be the readers of this short book. It's the inspiring story of a gentleman born in poverty who rose through education to a very high position in the medical field and then used his wisdom and financial means to lift up the village of his birth.

It's the story of Dr. Rodrigue Mortel, now a deacon according to the rites of the Roman Catholic Church.

Rodrigue was born in a small town of Haiti called St. Marc. He was born not in the center of the village but in the countryside. His illiterate mother—a first-class heroine—almost killed herself to provide an education to her boy. She walked to many marketplaces to sell all sorts of farm products. At one time she was expelled with her young family from the small house she rented because of her inability to pay the monthly due.

A woman of incredible faith, she pursued relentlessly her dream of providing a good education to her son.

After seven years of primary school at a Catholic School in St. Marc, Rodrigue was sent to Port-au-Prince where he successfully concluded his secondary classes. He then was admitted into the faculty of Medicine in Port-au-Prince. After graduation he worked in Haiti for a couple of years after which he was able to travel to the U.S., where he pursued his doctoral studies in this country, in Canada and in France. Thanks to his sharp intelligence and personal charm, he quickly became one of the most prominent professors at Penn State University, the associate dean and the founding director of the Cancer Center at Penn State.

However, this admirable story is not the focal point of this book. It's only its background. What is incredibly inspiring is what happened after his retirement.

Dr. Mortel went back to St. Marc and endeavored to provide his native village with an educational network that will make the journey to competency available to a forsaken population.

Using his own funds and whatever he could collect from a host of friends, he managed to build an elementary school for children from age three to twelve and then a secondary school for what would, more or less, correspond to four years of high school and the first two years of college in the U.S. Students are selected from the poorest families of the area.

What is of particular interest is the good doctor's efforts to emphasize **good character** alongside the thorough academic competency of the students. The students must learn integrity, social-mindedness, a passion to lift up the human level of the region. They must learn to trust in their ability to change the conditions of life of their compatriots. They must not be ashamed of their humble origin. Trust in God is paramount. The School is named **"Good Samaritans."** Students and teachers are called to emulate the moving dedication of the well-known Gospel story.

These radiating traits grant to this book a universal halo. What is said does not simply apply to Haiti but to the world. Knowledge can be used for good or bad purposes. Science is not a bloody tyrant but a great servant to mankind. Let science be used for the promotion of universal brotherhood!

Most Reverend Guy A. Sansaricq
Retired Auxiliary Bishop
Diocese of Brooklyn

CHAPTER ONE
FIRST FRUITS

Good Samaritans (Les Bons Samaritains)
Primary School

The harvest that July day was rich but small.

I stood before a sea of happy faces at the commencement for the first class to graduate from James Stine Collège in St. Marc, Haiti. Among the graduates were some of the students who had entered the primary school, Les Bons Samaritains (Good Samaritans), when it opened in 2001.

They were the first fruits of labors begun in the hope of bringing a new way of education to Haiti, the country of my birth; one that would unlock the potential of its people, so many of whom live in poverty and with little access to the means of bettering their lot.

The Few

Out of a starting group of sixty-five kindergarten students we accepted at Good Samaritans in 2001, only four made it to graduation from James Stine, the secondary school founded in 2011. The rest had dropped out, stayed behind or were asked to leave after failing to pass a repeated grade. Of the other students graduating from secondary school this day, most had come from other primary schools. Unlike the exclusively poor accepted into Good Samaritans, many of the students entering James Stine from other schools came from middle-class or even upper-class families. The evidence was glaring. The students from the other schools, who started earlier, outperformed ours who had started at age five.

At the practical level, our response to these results was already in the works: our new preschool, which would take children as young as three, was set to open in the next academic year; and the secondary school was offering remediation to keep struggling students from falling behind. At the conceptual level, the commitment to the project of reshaping education in Haiti would persist with renewed vigor.

As it was in my school days beginning in the 1940s, a full education in Haiti remains available to very few. Most Haitians will do anything to push their children to be educated. They know the value of education, but they cannot get it. My vision in founding Good Samaritans, followed by James Stine and three other schools for different purposes, was to create a model for education serving the poorest of the poor, one that if successful could be replicated across the country.

The four who had made it all the way through our program more than justified and vindicated this experiment in a different, more accessible form of education for Haitians. I was so proud of them, of how far they had come, and from where they had come. Their names and their stories stay with me.

Johnson Cirius we found in the street before enrolling in Good Samaritans. He did very well all the way through, always at the top of the class. In secondary school, he developed a particular interest in computer technology, which he pursued at university in Haiti. As of 2017, he had moved to the United States to study English in preparation for entering an American university.

Cedner Honorable was a bright student all around. He plans to study English at university in Haiti.

When we found him as a child, Josue Jean François had no mother but a father who worked occasional jobs. He is now in medical school in Port-au-Prince.

Roselanda Therzy always struck her teachers as being very intelligent but extremely shy, with little self-confidence. For a time after graduation, she remained at home because her family knew no one in Port-au-Prince to let her stay with them while studying at university there. Universities in Haiti generally do not provide dormitories, so students find apartments, which are very expensive, or they find families to take them in. Like many parents, Roselanda's were reluctant to send her to anyone they did not already know very well. In the fall of 2017, however, she began teaching at the preschool that we founded to support students even before coming to Good Samaritans.

Onward

Standing at that commencement podium with all this on my mind, I wanted to inspire the students to keep going. After congratulating them on their achievement, one that too few Haitians can claim, especially Haitians from poor backgrounds like theirs, I told them to think about the choice of a profession as their next mountain to climb. I had specific advice in mind for reaching certain of the summits arrayed before them:

Climb that mountain and become a physician if you have human compassion, the ability to alleviate pain, to help the sick, console the incurable and extract a smile from a dying patient. Climb it as an attorney if you have the ability to not only defend someone who is innocent even if he/she is poor but also resist the temptation to protect the criminal even if he/she is a millionaire. Climb that mountain as a judge if you feel you have the integrity and the moral courage of fairness that allows rulings without any taint of corruption. Climb it as a teacher if you have the ability to draw from your students the potential they did not know they had. Climb the mountain as a scientist if you have the ability to place your intellectual resources in the service of mankind. Climb it as a religious minister if you can use the pulpit to promote justice, love, honesty, and to preach against discrimination and dehumanization. Climb that mountain as a politician if you are willing to fight for human rights, provide equal opportunity to all groups, help citizens to preserve freedom, and place the welfare of the country above all else.

I also reminded them of the equipment they would need for scaling those heights—equipment that I hoped we had outfitted them with as part of their education: specifically, the character traits of honesty, integrity, productivity, assiduity, and determination. These were the habits of mind that my mother and the significant teachers in my life tried to instill in me from an early age and onward into my professional development. All of my experience pointed toward these traits as being the foundation for success in any career a student might choose.

Finally, I reminded the students that education not only opened opportunities but also placed an obligation to give to others as they themselves had received. I told them that "being an achiever doesn't make someone successful. There is indeed a big difference between the two. Personal accomplishments, your wealth, your rewards, and so on define an achiever, but a successful human being not only achieves but also helps along someone less fortunate."

I was eighty-one years old when I delivered those remarks, with most of my mountain summits at my back. The peak that still loomed before me was how to bring the benefits of education, by which I had been so blessed, to other people. "To whom much is given, much is required," as the Gospels so aptly put it.

The day reminded me most poignantly of the mountains I had climbed long ago to complete the education from which I had reaped great benefits, and also of the valley from which I had started, a valley just as deep as the one from which the poorest of the students sitting before me had come.

With these reminders came vivid flashbacks to another July day almost exactly twenty-five years earlier in 1989 when my mother died and was buried from a church just a stone's throw from where I stood at the podium. While I was almost giddy with joy throughout the commencement, I also felt most powerfully the sting of the loss of my mother, the prime mover behind so much of my own achievement and in whose memory I strove to bring these schools into being. She had worked herself to an extreme so that I could have something that eluded her all her life, much to her regret—the simple pleasures of reading and writing, the reward of a formal education.

Looking Back

Just like 40 percent of Haitians today[1] —and even more in my day—my mother and my father were totally illiterate. Primarily through the inspiration and example of my mother, I was able to complete primary school at L'Ecole Frère Herve in St. Marc, begin secondary school at Lycée Sténio Vincent, and finish at Lycée Tousaint Louverture in Port-au-Prince, then proceed to my professional degree at the Medical School of Port-au-Prince. I graduated from university in 1960 and completed two years of mandatory social service practicing in rural areas, before leaving Haiti

[1] The World Factbook, published by the Central Intelligence Agency (https://www.cia.gov/library/publications/the-world-factbook/geos/ha.html) Retrieved August 16, 2017.

in 1962, just as the regime of François "Papa Doc" Duvalier was taking a more oppressive turn.

After a year of graduate study in Montreal, I came to the United States for training in obstetrics/gynecology at Hahnemann Medical College and Hospital in Philadelphia, followed by specialization in gynecologic oncology at Memorial Sloan Kettering Cancer Center in New York. From there I joined the faculty of the Penn State College of Medicine, becoming chairman of the Department of Obstetrics and Gynecology in 1983, then moving to associate dean and founding director of the Penn State University Cancer Center. Along the way, there were several awards, many of them from Penn State throughout my career there and beyond. Among my most cherished honors was the Horatio Alger Award in 1985, given by the Horatio Alger Association of Distinguished Americans to outstanding Americans who have succeeded in spite of adversity, and with an emphasis on the importance of higher education. That award would describe my later mission in life and my hope for the students our schools have educated.

After my retirement in 2001, I took on a whole new calling, though it had been several years in the making. I was ordained a permanent deacon in the Catholic Church after commuting from my home in Hershey, Pennsylvania, for three years of study at St. Mary's Seminary in Baltimore. In addition to serving in parishes, I became director of the Missions Office of the Archdiocese of Baltimore, a vantage point particularly helpful in pressing my strategy for improving education in Haiti through cooperation and exchange between the archdiocese in my adopted country and the Diocese of Gonaïves in my mother country.

The point of this book, then, is to present a blueprint for others who share this vision to transform Haiti through education. This story points to but a few of the resources available among churches, foundations, and other institutions, as well as vast reservoirs of goodwill among individuals willing to help. In my experience, people and institutions are just waiting to be asked. All my fellow visionaries need to mobilize them behind a new vision is character, credibility, and an attractive plan. This book shows how it can be done, with the hope that it will be done to transform education in Haiti and bring new opportunities to young people.

Epiphanies

Before diving into the details of how to found schools in Haiti, it may help to explain certain early experiences that inspired this vision and pushed me to make it a reality. Two events stand out—one a searing memory from childhood, the other a chance encounter in my professional life. Growing up in St. Marc, my sister and I were "natural" children, as they call those born out of wedlock. When I was very young, going to Mass regularly and serving as an altar boy, I wanted to become a priest. But the seminary in those days would not take candidates whose parents were unmarried, so I was partly responsible for my parents' decision to marry when I was eleven years old. To get married though, they had to go through the sacrament in church and hold a large reception afterward, as was the custom. Whatever they had, which was not much, they spent on the wedding. As a result, they could not pay the rent, which was about four dollars a month at the time. We were evicted. Watching this, I did not know quite what was going on, but I saw a member of the city government come and put our furniture out on the street. For this paltry sum, the whole family was driven out of our home and into the streets for lack of payment, right before the beginning of the school year. As this scene was unfolding, my mother, who was crying, said, "If I had had an education, this would not have happened."

Although we quickly found temporary accommodations and later, through my mother's hard work, owned a home, that anguished sentence of hers has stayed with me. The day of the eviction was when I made the decision to go as high as I could. I determined that wherever I go, and in whatever I undertake, I want to be at the top. By the time my parents got around to marrying, by the way, I had changed my career aspirations from celebrating the sacraments to flying airplanes as a commercial pilot.

It was only a bit later that I sensed my vocation to medicine, and this, too, stemmed more from my ambition than my actual interests at the time. In secondary school, as the top student in math, I was leaning toward a career in engineering. But medical school was the hardest to get into, accepting only forty applicants each year, no matter how many applied. Some years the acceptance rate dipped below 10 percent. Medicine was by far the most prestigious of the professions. Despite my initial concerns about confronting a cadaver in anatomy class, medical school is where I applied, and was accepted, after a summer of crash study, sleeping only every other day. The memory of the eviction experience kept coming back to me every time I thought about what I could give to Haiti and its people.

The other pivot point came in the 1970s while I was teaching at Penn State and the head of my department expressed an interest in traveling with me to Haiti and learning more about it. So we went. While spending an afternoon on a beach, we met two nurses who said they had come from Switzerland to work at Albert Schweitzer Hospital. Though I had never visited this place before, I had heard much about it. Larimer Mellon, Jr., heir to a family banking and oil fortune in Pittsburg, had founded the hospital in 1956 after deciding to follow the example of Albert Schweitzer and spend the rest of his life as a medical missionary. Just as Albert Schweitzer had done in leaving behind a musical career in Europe to start what became a world-famous hospital in the African nation of Gabon, Dr. Mellon had enlisted the aid of the Haitian government and invested a large part of his fortune to open the hospital in the Artibonite river valley, about sixty miles northwest of Port-au-Prince. The valley continues today as a rice-producing region that is very rural and poor, little changed from when my mother's family lived there.

After learning who we were—two physicians from a prominent American university—the Swiss nurses invited us to come see Albert Schweitzer Hospital. Upon arriving, we found the wife of a third-year medical resident from America going through the tenth hour of childbearing labor, seemingly unable to deliver. The nearest obstetrician was in Port-au-Prince, which was too far away. But here we were—two obstetricians. This was providential! We delivered a boy who has since grown up to be a cardio-thoracic surgeon practicing in Arizona.

The experience affected me deeply because there were so many people in the United States who could do what I do, but in Haiti, there was such a need. Dr. Mellon said at the time, "Come back whenever you want. The hospital is yours." And so I did.

Resolve

After that fortuitous visit with Dr. Mellon, I started spending half my annual four weeks of vacation helping in medical practice in Haiti, supplementing that drawn-out benevolence with donations of medical equipment and supplies (antibiotics, gowns, suture sets, x-ray machine, and so on) to Albert Schweitzer as well as the local hospital in St. Marc.

My attraction to philanthropic endeavors was confirmed and encouraged during visits to other developing countries as, subliminally, whenever taking such a tour I always saw a better Haiti through the prism of other, better-administered countries. A vivid case was Costa Rica, which shares the same climate as my homeland but has a literacy rate of nearly 100 percent.[2] Needless to say, Costa Rica is far more advanced economically.

As much as I enjoyed doing volunteer work at Albert Schweitzer Hospital, something was gnawing at my entrails to find a way to reach more folks and on a more permanent basis. From my experience as a country doctor for two years after graduation from medical school, it had become painfully obvious that there was plenty of pathology among the public. Many times in the past, I had felt impotent when facing the sick because I did not have the technical means at my disposal to take care of

---

[2] The World Factbook, published by the Central Intelligence Agency
(https://www.cia.gov/library/publications/the-world-factbook/geos/cs.html)
Retrieved September 14, 2017.

their medical needs. I was elated to be of use at Albert Schweitzer. I was elated as a native son to come back, after training at prestigious academic centers in the United States, to humbly serve my less fortunate brothers and sisters. But it bothered me that many volunteers who were helping were not even native people.

Dr. Mellon's initial invitation to me was no less than an epiphany. From that epiphany came study and analysis, and the conclusion that if I was to do anything in aid of my beloved motherland, all of the available evidence was pointing clearly in one, and only one, direction: education, education, education.

CHAPTER TWO
POOR NEIGHBORHOOD, RICH CHILDHOOD

St. Marc, Haiti

I had acquired an education, a priceless one that I can attribute to both personal factors as well as cultural ones, having grown up in what is widely regarded as a golden era of Haitian culture. To understand how I came to my education, and my desire to pass along the benefits, it is important to know something of the milieu that formed me, and where I conceived and pursued my early ambitions.

Family Life

St. Marc is a city on Haiti's west coast, part of the Artibonite Department (each of Haiti's ten provinces is known as a department). The Artibonite River divides the department between a mountainous region in the north and a flat river valley in the south, where St. Marc is located. The city sprawls beyond an urban core to five rural sections within its jurisdiction. My father and mother came from these outer sections to find work in the city proper, which easily accommodated its population of twenty-five thousand when I was a child there in the 1930s and '40s. At that time, the society was very elite professionally, culturally, and socially. Even though my family took no part in this elite, St. Marc was a pleasant place to live for most of its inhabitants. It was a place where my mother, for example, could find opportunity for herself, despite the severe disadvantages under which she labored. I start with her because she was the one who served as my unique inspiration—and example—to achieve.

My mother was born Lamercie Antoine, the only daughter of a family of six children, in a rural section of St. Marc called Savary. Her parents were peasants who grew rice and searched for a better way of life for their daughter. Unable to pay for her education, they sought the help of a notable family some distance away in the central city. The family promised to send my mother to school if she came to live with them. Instead of a classroom, my mom entered hell. The host family used my mother to do all the household chores, including taking care of their children, never thinking for one minute to honor the promise to send her to school. She became part of the child-labor system, a form of slavery really, known as *restavek*, which prevails in some parts of Haiti even today. Ironically, this occurs in the same society that prides itself as the first in modern times to break the bondage of slavery, led by Haiti's liberators and heroes, Toussaint Louverture and Jean-Jacques Dessalines, who won independence from France in 1804.

As a result, my mother grew up illiterate and remained so for all her life. Still, she was one of the smartest and wisest persons I have ever met. She suffered no lack of self-esteem, never cowered in response to adversity. Instead, she became a pillar of our community, with a reputation for common sense and a strong work ethic.

My mother finally left the bondage of *restavek* when she met my father, Demarant Mortel. He, however, was different from my mother in almost every respect. He never did anything to stimulate me. He was not ambitious. Working as a tailor, he served only the people in the rural area, not those in town who could afford better. He was just there, usually playing cards. At night he turned his shop into an informal gambling club, taking a cut from the pot of the card games played there. I have long ago forgiven him because I came to realize that he also had an unpleasant childhood. He was born out of wedlock and when his mom married another man, the man chose not to adopt my father or send him to school. Retaining his mom's maiden name, my father was made to feel very much like the stepchild he was.

So it was my mother primarily who provided for the family, both before and after our eviction by the landlord. She worked as a rice vendor, buying rice fresh from the harvest in the rural river valley and hauling it by public truck transport to a milling facility in downtown St. Marc. There my mother would enlist me in the three-day drying process, spreading the rice on the pavement before it could be milled and bagged for public truck transport again, this time to the train station. With the bags of rice stowed on board, my mother and other women like her embarked on the daylong railway journey to the big, open-air markets of Port-au-Prince. With little else to do during the trip, the band of vendors talked, and talked. They became known as the "madan sara," after a bird that sings all time, just as these women talked through the long journey and as they sat in the marketplace.

Once in the city, my mother would unload the bags in the market, and the bags would remain there until all the rice was sold. There was no place to secure them at night, so my mother and the other vendors would sleep in the market next to their merchandise, with a tarp hung overhead for when it rained. They lived outdoors, exposed to whatever weather and with little access to running water. My mother would leave for Port-au-Prince on Monday morning and return on Saturday. Waiting to see my mom on weekends was the highlight of my week. She played the role of both parents.

Our household included my parents, my older sister Dinah, two cousins, and me. As was common, even the poorest helped each other. As bad as her financial position was, my mother took it upon herself to raise her two nieces as her own daughters. She taught me that if there were enough to feed two mouths, then there would be enough for four mouths. I saw this mentality play out again and again with peasants I would encounter later on. Life in those days was hard but not bitter. I was born into poverty but it did not define me.

Just as important, my mom instilled in me the love of God. She never missed Sunday Mass when she was home and always made sure I came along. It was a matter of pride for me to please my mother and to emulate her. Although financially poor, she was spiritually rich and honest to a fault. Her word was gold; she never went back on it. Her pride would not allow her to do so.

In theory, I had all the elements of failure in life, but my mother would never let that happen regardless of the cost. She always encouraged me to excel in school. She never doubted for a minute I had what it would take to succeed.

Foremost among my mother's sacrifices was ensuring that I attended Catholic schools from the very beginning. My first school was a public school, built by the government, but handed over for operation by the Christian Brothers, a Catholic religious order devoted to educating young people, particularly among the poor. As a public school, it was open for anyone to apply but the spaces were limited, so admission was competitive. The year before applying, I had gone to a preschool where we learned to read a little. This helped because when the Christian

Brothers interviewed the student candidates, they asked them to read aloud. Fortunately, I was able to read enough to get in.

Never Bored

For poor youngsters, there was not much formal entertainment on offer, but through imagination and improvisation, the possibilities were endless. At school during breaks, my friends and I played soccer, but at home on weekends or during vacation, we had no standard ball to play with. So we used whatever was round and available. More often than not, this was an orange (the sour type being most suitable), tightly rolled socks, or occasionally a tennis ball. We played barefoot on the unpaved streets, for it was absolutely forbidden to play ball in regular shoes lest we tear them. Injuries to toes often resulted, though typically we kept playing because the pressure to join a game was too much to resist.

I vividly remember a time when I was about nine when I injured my toe and kept playing, with the aid of cotton leaf dressing on it. That night I developed horrible pain, waking my parents with my hollering. Upon inspecting the toe with a flashlight, they discovered and removed a worm. The pain subsided immediately, and I was able to go back to sleep.

Another favored pastime of my youth was swimming at the beaches that graced our coastal city. For organized picnics, the best place was Grosse Roche, about fifteen minutes away by car. For boys too young to drive, and who had no other access to cars, it was best to walk the shorter distances to the Wharf and Kay William. After competing to see who could swim the farthest or the fastest, my friends and I roasted conches on the beach. I nearly drool today at the memory of those feasts.

Not all of the entertainment was pure frolic. As teenagers, my friends and I enjoyed visiting the courthouse in St. Marc to listen to trial lawyers pleading. We learned the names of the best of them—Kénol, Sabala, and Legros. They stood out as orators in a Francophone tradition that prizes an elaborate eloquence. I still have sentences running through my head from these trials—many of them spoken by lawyers insulting the judge. A lot of people in my class went into law. I think the courthouse spectating had a lot to do with it.

In all these activities, we made do and found ways to have fun. Boredom was never an option.

Learning from the Best, the Eccentric

Meanwhile, I was being educated by a variety of teachers and interesting characters, many of them memorable, though for different reasons.

During secondary school, my Latin teacher was so dull, my friends and I would cut his classes to swim in the local river. My behavior changed, however, as I started studying literature and the humanities, spending hours memorizing whole passages of texts. My favorites were the seventeenth-century French classics such as Corneille, and Racine. To this day, I can still recite most of Corneille's.

An unforgettable secondary school teacher, Antoine Carré, taught philosophy. He had studied in France, only to return with a pompous air about him. A most comical figure, he would begin class with a witticism, on one occasion telling us: "Aristotle is dead, Descartes is dead, Pascal and Kant have passed away and yours truly doesn't feel well." To which one of the brighter students retorted, "Are you then implying you deserve to be mentioned in the same breath as such august men?" Without missing a beat, Carré replied, "Some people take pleasure in saying so."

Carré we mocked. But another philosophy teacher, Professor Gilbert, whom my classmates and I sought out while preparing for the national baccalaureate exam, we revered. Students from schools all over Port-au-Prince crowded his lectures. Proceeding in a humble style, he would deconstruct a narrative, synthesize apparently unrelated concepts, challenge and buffet one's mind while impressing with the clarity or the cleverness of an argument.

A similar mix of brilliance and eccentricity continued in my education at medical school.

There was Professor Kébreau whose students clapped at the end of his lectures, so much so that he would let us know which area to concentrate on for a test, depending on the amount of applause he would get.

Professor Dallemand, on the other hand, would bring a book and just read from it without any explanation of the material. If he knew the subject matter apart from the text, he did not let on. Buoyed by a political atmosphere filled with protest after the fall of President Paul Magloire's government, students started demanding better performance from their teachers. In that spirit, we wrote Professor Dallemand a note asking him to stop teaching and left it on his desk. Opening the note the next day just before lecture, he burst into tears and left the university for good. Although I did not care for the professor's teaching method, on a human level it was a painful spectacle to watch. We should have found a less public, more diplomatic way. Such brash behavior was an unfortunate part of my youth and inexperience, particularly at that politically charged time in Haiti.

Philosophy classes had a serious impact on me even as I began concentrating in the hard sciences. I vividly remember some of my essays. At the national exams at the end of secondary school, I wrote an exegesis on Claude Bernard's saying, *"La véritable méthode de la science expérimentale est le doute."* (My translation: "Doubt is the best method for experimental scientific inquiry.") Without realizing it then, the groundwork was being laid for my future approach to scientific inquiry. Doubt as I see it is healthy but not all-encompassing. It plays a determining role in scientific study without necessarily negating faith in the spiritual realm and religious matters.

Cosmopolitan Influence

During this golden era in Haiti, Port-au-Prince became world-renowned. In 1949, the Exposition Internationale du Bicentenaire was held there to mark two hundred years since its founding. That year and for years after, thousands of tourists flocked to the city to savor our culture. The harbor area, named Bicentenaire, specifically built for the expo, included a multicolored waterfall. Concerts recorded there often synchronized the music with its flow.

Nearby was the Théâtre de Verdure, an amphitheater where memorable performances were staged, ranging from dramas such as "Adieu à la Marseillaise," about Toussaint Louverture, to acts such as Theodore Beaubrun, Haiti's foremost comedian, who interpreted daily life in Haiti through his character, "Languichatte" (which translates to "cat's tongue"). For open-air concerts featuring musicians touring from other countries, and for soccer games as well, Magloire Stadium was the grand venue. And every week, military bands played martial tunes and classical music in the Champ de Mars, a large public square in the heart of the city. The square doubled as a study hall by night as students who lacked electricity in their living quarters gathered under its lampposts to read. I joined that studious throng every early morning before class and every evening afterward during the school year.

Despite the lively concert scene, however, our own music was seldom heard on the radio, the main exception being the radio DJ popularly called Zo who pushed for Haitian music and spoke primarily in our own Creole vernacular. Otherwise, Cuban salsa was the most popular, followed by Mexican ranchera and French love songs. Because of Port-au-Prince's reputation and our infatuation with Latin music, Cuban and Mexican artists made a point of performing in Port-au-Prince. Prominent among them were the Cuban luminaries Perez Prado, known as "King of the Mambo," and Celia Cruz, known as the "Queen of Salsa."

Another popular radio announcer was Antoine Hérard. A French-speaking orator, he used to announce the play-by-play of soccer games, the official ceremonies of the government and so on. Radio was the main medium for entertainment. TV was still in the distant future.

Crime was virtually unheard of then. Personal security was not a concern. The plague of drug trafficking was still far off.

Clouds began to form in 1957 when Duvalier came to power. Curfews were imposed and political assemblies banned in the population centers. Even a public gathering for my university graduation was forbidden. My classmates and I had to receive our diplomas privately, without the usual fanfare. Our reaction to these changes was to look back into our history and find new outlets for public expression. We ended up reviving and amplifying the public celebration of Mardi Gras. If we could not gather for political purposes, at least we could crowd the streets for a religious celebration—a party—in advance of Ash Wednesday and the onset of Lent.

Fast forward to today. St. Marc has nearly two hundred thousand people, though its infrastructure has changed little since it held a population of twenty-five thousand. You see rural people migrating to St. Marc for new opportunities, leaving behind antiquated agricultural methods and lack of schools. In response, many of the elite people of the city move out to Port-au-Prince. These new people in St. Marc are not educated. These are people who urinate in public, who throw trash in the street, who rummage through garbage. Driving along the main boulevard is now dangerous. Motorcycle taxis carrying as many as five people at a time weave in and out of the traffic, cutting people off, and causing accidents.

Of course, I speak about my hometown wistfully, as a native who remembers better. Visitors from the outside tend to find their senses overloaded by the sights. Beth Hough, a teacher from Archbishop Spalding High School in Severn, Maryland, who volunteered for a week at Good Samaritans in 2017, saw downtown St. Marc this way: "Trash litters most of the streets, there is still no sewage system, and there are animals roaming free everywhere you look. I am not talking about cats and dogs, but goats, pigs, and roosters. Men on scooters fill the streets, moving in orderly chaos—no traffic lights or stop signs, just unspoken rules of the road. Honking horns sound everywhere, from early morning until well into the night."

Fortunately, for her and for us, Mrs. Hough also saw our Good Samaritans school as an oasis in the middle of it all.

Another visitor from America who volunteered at the school was Marvin Roxas. One of the first students to take part in an Archdiocese of Baltimore mission trip to Haiti, he was struck by the contrasts. "I see a land of disparity and contradictions," he wrote on our school website, offering his first impressions. "I see run-down shacks and trash-filled, unpaved roads overshadowed by majestic mountains. I see beautiful Haitian people living in houses without running water, food, or electricity. And I see the glorious sunset over washing waves as a homeless man shows me his mangled hands when he begs for food."

Indeed, there is noise and poverty, as well as great beauty in the land and in its people. This is what a subculture of illiteracy is like, where great potential does not find its full flowering. My education experiment is being conducted in these conditions.

CHAPTER THREE
EDUCATION IN HAITI— THE PROBLEM

Haitian Students

As I have pointed out, most Haitians will do anything for an education for their children; actually providing one is another matter. The system favors a few and pushes them very far. Those few who rise to university receive a very broad education, typically achieving fluent writing proficiency in French, English, and Spanish. For the great majority left behind, however, several factors—economic, cultural, and structural—impede progress in their formal learning.

A few statistics will help introduce the problem.

For me, the most troubling of these numbers describe the various levels of illiteracy in the country. About 40 percent of adults are illiterate.[1] In many cases, this occurs despite attendance at school. Some three-quarters of children completing first grade, and about half those completing second grade, do so without being able to read a single word.[2]

For many families, access to any school at all is problematic. A recent survey among youth ages fifteen to twenty-four in Haiti revealed more than 40 percent had not completed primary school education.[3] Of these, 4 percent had received no formal education at all.[4]

The system of national examinations, for which pass rates are low, eventually narrows the flow of students through the grade levels to barely a trickle. The pass rate for students taking exams in the sixth year of school is about 75 percent. For those who move on to the ninth year of education, the pass rate is about 70 percent. For students who reach secondary school, the pass rate for graduation and a chance at entering university has consistently run around 30 percent.[5] Remember, these pass rates apply to the already winnowed group of students who have progressed beyond primary school.

Several factors underlie this failure in education. Poverty, government corruption, and vulnerability to natural disasters—most recently the earthquake of 2010 and Hurricane Matthew in 2016, each of which produced a national crisis—stand in the way of sustained economic investment and growth. Given the chance, Haitians do very well for themselves in other countries, mostly in the United States and Canada, just not so well in their own country. Remittances of money from Haitians

---

[1] Education Fact Sheet, March 2017, USAID.
[2] Ibid.
[3] National Education Profile, 2014 Update, World Bank.
[4] Ibid.
[5] "Exam Results Disappointing, the Minister Manigat Announced a Package of Measures," Haiti Libre, October 8, 2014. (https://www.haitilibre.com/en/news-11781-haiti-education-exam-results-disappointing-the-minister-manigat-announced-a-package-of-measures.html)

living and working abroad, sent to their relatives back home, represent more than a quarter of gross domestic product. Unemployment and underemployment are widespread; more than two-thirds of those in the labor force lack formal jobs. Nearly 60 percent of its people live below the national poverty line. Not surprisingly, Haiti is ranked the poorest country in the Western Hemisphere.[6]

This poverty looks different from what you see in the United States, or in most other Western countries. Basic necessities are lacking. The toilet is an outhouse. For running water, a family typically sends a child once or twice a week, during the times of day when the pipes are flowing, to fetch water in containers from a public spigot. Most families live in dwellings of one or two rooms. Sometimes the crowding is such that family members must take turns sleeping. It has changed little since my youth.

School Structures

Next, consider the education structure itself in Haiti. Theoretically, education starts in preschool for children ages three to five, followed by what is called Fundamental Education for nine grades, then four years of secondary school.

Schools divide roughly into four basic categories: (1) private schools run by religious groups, mostly Catholic religious orders, though some Protestant missions as well; (2) schools organized in buildings built and owned by the government but contracted out to religious organizations and also private, non-religious programs; (3) entirely private schools run by lay people, which can vary significantly in quality, depending on who is running them; and (4) entirely public, government-run schools.

Approximately 85 percent of all schools in Haiti fall into these first three, privately-run categories.[7] The first two—private religious schools

---

[6] The World Factbook, published by the Central Intelligence Agency (https://www.cia.gov/library/publications/the-world-factbook/geos/ha.html) Retrieved August 16, 2017.
[7] Education Fact Sheet, March 2017, USAID.

and private schools working on contract with the government—perform at a consistently high level. The bottom two are largely ineffective.

Elements of the third category—typically unaccredited, non-religious private schools—tend to be strictly in the business of making money, regardless of the results among the children. I call them "grocery schools" because of the strictly commercial nature of the exchange between parent and school, with the school exploiting the unsuspecting, often illiterate parents. The parents do not realize until it too late that they have paid scarce money to a school that cannot advance the education of their children.

Only students from accredited schools may take the national exam that students must pass to enter into secondary school, and most of these grocery schools are unaccredited. That being the case, many of these schools send their graduating eighth-graders to accredited private schools for ninth grade in order to qualify for the exam. But the inadequacy of preparation in the first eight years of school is usually too great for the transferring students to overcome in a single year. Students from the grocery schools may take the exam two or three times without passing, and then drop out. These schools produce a different kind of literacy—not total illiteracy but functional illiteracy.

The entirely public schools are not much better, mainly because they pay teachers irregularly. The government may pay for one month after three or four months of teaching. When the payment is late, many teachers will not show up to class. Often they are people who have friends in the government so they cannot be fired.

Some teachers study pedagogy in university. Otherwise, anyone who passes the baccalaureate exam at the end of secondary school can become a teacher. You don't have to study education in order to teach. For many teachers, teaching in Haiti is not a vocation; it is just a job.

Across all four categories of schools, the teaching itself relies mainly on rote methods. Because of the national testing required to enter secondary school, and then university, teachers tend to "teach to the test."

In Haiti it is all memory. Critical thinking is not developed. You have to pass an exam; that is critical. There is very little opportunity to add much to round out the curriculum. Schools may continue to teach something that was so in 1900, even if it is different now more than a century later.

Most school facilities are sparsely furnished, typically with just an individual desk and chair for the teacher, a blackboard, and benches and writing tables for the students facing the teacher. Some of these bare classrooms are crowded with as many as a hundred students. As far as extracurricular activity—nothing, no library, no science lab, no computers. In the better public and private schools run by religious organizations, you start to see more. Even in Catholic schools, which are among the best, 57 percent lack potable water, 38 percent lack water suitable for hand washing. On the tech front, not just a dearth of resources but an irregular electrical grid impairs even these better schools. Only 7 percent of Catholic schools in Haiti have internet access and just 20 percent have one or more computers.[8] Among the schools that do have computers many must charge the students extra for them.

For a great many students, though, the choices are more basic. If they have to buy books, then they cannot buy clothes. Their families may not be able to afford to send them to private school, or even public school.

Thus, the education system in Haiti affords little access to the poor. A few can be highly educated, but most of those who have any education at all have a very mediocre one. After graduation, there may not be a place to work. Much of the employment is with the government.

Cultural Factors

Many of the cultural barriers to education in Haiti are grounded in economic problems; that is, poverty and the limitations it imposes. But one, language, is purely cultural. Until the beginning of this century, all

---

[8] Final Report of The National Survey of Catholic Schools in Haiti, The Episcopal Commission for Catholic Education, Catholic Relief Services and the University of Notre Dame, June, 2012 (https://ace.nd.edu/files/haiti/Consulting_HaitiForumReport.pdf)

schools in Haiti taught exclusively in French, not in Creole, which is the common language that emerged and developed among African slaves imported to Haiti during the French colonial era. In my time you got punished if you spoke Creole in the classroom even though Creole is what you spoke at home and on the street. The elite speak French, but the non-elite speak Creole. Nowadays, in response to recent changes in government policy, primary schools generally teach the reading and writing of Creole two hours a week and French five to seven hours a week. Still, the problem is that you learn in French but you speak in Creole. You have a math problem; it is written in French but you have to go to Creole in your mind to work it out.

Geography presents another problem. As of 2015, nearly 40 percent of the population was concentrated in rural areas, many of them isolated.[9] Children from these settlements may have to walk a long distance each way to attend a rural school, which is usually a government school. Once there, however, the child also needs to be fed. If you do not feed them, you may not see them again. Or if they do come back, they are sleeping or they cannot absorb anything you teach them because they are hungry and tired.

To compensate, some families arrange for their children to stay with friends or relatives who live near schools, or near better schools than those nearby. This means that in a poor family, which is the great majority, parents must be selective as to which of their children to educate, and possibly to send out of the home to live with someone else close to the nearest available school. Parents will push the boys to go anywhere, but most will not push the girl outside the house without knowing more about the quality of the person she will be living with. In Haiti, many young people stay home with their parents till they marry.

Some of those living-away arrangements fall into the *restavek* tra-

---

[9] The World Factbook, published by the Central Intelligence Agency (https://www.cia.gov/library/publications/the-world-factbook/geos/ha.html) Retrieved August 16, 2017

dition that trapped my mother into virtual slavery at a young age and effectively deprived her of an education. Even when the host family does make gestures toward fulfilling its side of the bargain, the child's obligation to perform household chores takes precedence. Quite simply, if the children do not finish their chores on time, they do not go to school.

Another inhibition to schooling in Haiti arises from what would otherwise count as a strength if the Haitian economy were developed to a more sophisticated level. Here I speak of the informal commercial instincts of the people. Just as my mother used to buy raw rice in the country and mill it for sale in the city, many Haitians still today would forgo steady work for this life of trading on marginal differences between separate markets. Everybody is moving; everybody is selling something. They might buy a hundred pens from a factory and sell them on the street one pen at a time. How much benefit can you make selling ten pens? These are small margins, and you cannot live on them. Pursuing this type of livelihood, you can never go from one step to the next in the economy. The allure of the easy entry into this form of commerce is another factor in drawing young people away from pursuing a higher level of education.

Yet this way of life is preferred. I see it at the house I built next to Good Samaritans, where I stay during my regular visits there. I engage people to clean it and watch over it while I am living in my primary residence in the United States. But after two or three months working for me in St. Marc, these caretakers leave and spend all their money over six months, usually buying something in bulk to sell individually on the streets.

Haitians' love of small-time commerce sometimes creates an inflated sense of what we can do without expertise, without education. You ask someone to build a piece of furniture. Can you do it? Of course, comes the reply. But the result is totally different from what you asked. In illiterate segments of society, people try to bluff their way to opportunity.

In resolving to do something about these problems, starting with

Good Samaritans in my home region of the Artibonite river valley, I sensed myself becoming a willing participant in a providential master plan that is as simple as it is eternal, and therefore powerful. The cycle of life revolves around the idea of the balance of giving and receiving. Once one tastes the blessing of being helped, one must reciprocate in due time.

CHAPTER FOUR
THE VISION:
A NEW GENERATION

Bishop Emmanuel Constant, Rodrigue Mortel,
and Cardinal William Keeler

More than any specific design for a new school and curriculum for Haiti, what I had at first was a vision for empowering Haitians through educa-tion. It was, and remains, nothing less than the formation of a new gen-eration of Haitians. Using a holistic approach to accomplish it, I would want to instill in their very fiber the love of God, country, and countrymen. These would be the necessary qualities to become a new breed of leaders, capable of steering the country in a new path.

The Troika

While the vision was mine, the details of realizing it gradually fell into place by many twists and turns of seemingly providential origin, working substantially through two influential relationships, one formed in Haiti and the other in the United States.

When I moved from St. Marc to Port-au-Prince to complete secondary school and stayed on for medical school, I eventually made friends with my neighborhood parish pastor, the Rev. Emmanuel Constant; it was a friendship that continued until his death in 2009. We lost touch somewhat during my early years in the United States but renewed our ties in the 1970s when I started returning to the country to volunteer at the Albert Schweitzer Hospital. By that time, he had become Bishop Constant of the Diocese of Gonaïves, whose boundaries follow those of the Artibonite Department (in Haiti, each Catholic diocese is geographically coextensive with the department in which it is located).

The second relationship formed through an even more unlikely happenstance, this time through a public stand on the abortion issue. When I became chairman of the Obstetrics-Gynecology Department at Penn State in 1983, one of my first decisions was to force the separation from the department of an attending physician who used to do twelve abortions there every Tuesday. It has long been part of my core belief that terminating a pregnancy is tantamount to destroying a life. In my heart, and in my head as a physician, I could not conceive of it. I do not see the matter in political terms. I am a man of faith and my faith guides me and tells me not to interfere with a natural process. Life is sacred and not to be tampered with.

The decision drew both wrath and admiration. From the local chapter of Planned Parenthood came the threat of a lawsuit. From Bishop William H. Keeler, then the bishop of the Diocese of Harrisburg, Pennsylvania, came an invitation to meet. When we got together, Bishop Keeler praised my public stand for Catholic principle, and in the wide-ranging conversation that followed, we entered a friendship that would last until his death in 2017. For many years the bishop joined my family and me for Easter Sunday meals, alternating between my house in Hershey and his residence in Harrisburg.

Planned Parenthood never followed through with the lawsuit, which could have diverted huge swaths of time and money from my professional progress and my eventual plans for Haiti. That it did not happen bears out what I often say as a deacon giving homilies at mass: when you are doing the work of God, if it is the right thing to do, just let it happen. Do not worry about the outcome.

As my friendship with Bishop Keeler grew, so did his interest in my native land. I introduced him to Bishop Constant. They became friends, and Bishop Keeler invited him to preach on several occasions for the annual missions' event in which each American Catholic diocese invites clergy from another country to spend time in the diocese engaging in cultural exchange and seeking support for missions in the home country. When Bishop Keeler was appointed in 1989 to lead the Archdiocese of Baltimore (where he was later elevated to cardinal), he brought with him a love for Haiti in his heart. The three of us became what I think of as a troika pulling Baltimore and Haiti together, to the benefit of both.

The alliance with these two clerics was essential to the success of my project. If you want to accomplish something lasting in Haiti, you do not want to associate with the government because it is always changing and often not fully respected. Instead, the Catholic Church is the institution in Haiti that has the infrastructure at both the local and national levels.

Although many other religious organizations and secular non-governmental organizations (NGOs) carry out significant missions in Haiti, they do not have the same reach and internal coordination as the Church in what remains a culturally Catholic country. Working with the Church is to have a partner that is constant and powerful. Nearly the entire country was Catholic when I was growing up; now the official figure is 54.7 percent of the population identifying as Catholic and nearly all the rest belonging to various Protestant traditions.[1] Still, the Church in Haiti remains widely respected and continues to generate good ideas in its social ministries, though it may lack the resources to launch them all. With its global reach—to the Archdiocese of Baltimore and the Diocese of Harrisburg, just for example—the Church is able to accomplish much more than it would otherwise. To me, this is the ideal marriage of vision and resources.

Perhaps the first such initiative of our working troika—albeit on a much smaller scale—took the form of the two bishops collaborating to help me seek ordination to the permanent diaconate in the Catholic Church. There were procedural obstacles to overcome. Archbishop Keeler's successor in the Diocese of Harrisburg, where I lived then and still do today, had discontinued the permanent diaconate program there. The Archdiocese of Baltimore had a program, but it imposed an age limit. Candidates had to be young enough to complete their studies and reach ordination by the age of sixty, a milestone I had already passed. The plan then shifted to the Diocese of Gonaïves, which had no permanent deacon program either but did have a bishop willing to accommodate my new calling. My two mitered friends agreed that Bishop Constant would ordain me in Gonaïves but entrust my formation for ministry to Archbishop Keeler in Baltimore.

So, I enrolled in the permanent diaconate program at St. Mary's Seminary in Baltimore in 1998, making a ninety-minute commute on Saturdays from my home in Hershey. The rigors of the curriculum began sorting out the candidates within the first few months. Out of an initial class of fifteen, only six of us were ordained in 2001.

Like many of the men studying with me, I had a day job, a very

---

[1] The World Factbook, published by the Central Intelligence Agency
(https://www.cia.gov/library/publications/the-world-factbook/geos/ha.html)
Retrieved November 28, 2017.

demanding one as chairman of my department and later director of the Penn State Cancer Center. Yet my planning for some kind of education project—still in formation—continued apace. An early step was to create the Mortel Family Charitable Foundation in 1997, funded initially with $25,000 of my own. This foundation, together with a separate companion entity formed in 2016, would go on to solicit donations in support of the capital and operating expenses of my educational venture.

Soon after I enrolled in the diaconate program, Cardinal Keeler and Bishop Constant named their respective jurisdictions as sister dioceses under a Baltimore/Haiti Project of mutual support and religious and cultural exchange. In Baltimore, the program was administered by the Office of the Propagation of the Faith—later changed to simply, the Office of Missions—headed by Msgr. Victor Galeone, who would soon become another source of encouragement in my efforts.

Becoming a Reality

With the Mortel Family Foundation up and running, other pieces of the puzzle started falling into place.

The school, if there was to be one, needed experienced teachers. In 1998, a year after forming the foundation, I turned to the Sisters of St. Joseph de Cluny, a Catholic religious order that operated schools in South America and the Caribbean, including the best girls' school in Haiti. Within a month of meeting the provincial of the order in Haiti and submitting my proposal, I received a letter of approval at the local level but with a caution that it had to be submitted to headquarters in Paris. To my pleasant surprise two weeks later, a letter came back with effusive praise for the project and a positive answer. It was a surprise because the Sisters of St. Joseph de Cluny had the reputation—undeserved as it turned out—of catering to the well-off, and my project was for the poor.

The next pleasant surprise was an offer I could not have dreamed of—though I had been working on it for some time—to purchase land for the school. As far back as the early 1990s, I had been thinking about the right location for a school, starting with possibly converting our family house in St. Marc to classrooms, though that idea was soon discarded as impractical. In 1993, I had purchased ten acres from a major landowner just outside the urban core, with the intent of building a school there. But the area was difficult to access by public transportation and surrounded by development of a lavish, upscale neighborhood, all of which was inappropriate and too much culture shock for very young children stepping out from their poverty for the first time.

Now, just as I was ready to start the school, I learned that a cousin of mine who lived in Florida but still owned a large parcel of land wanted to sell it to a local person. It was in the urban core, less than a mile but a world away from the plot I had purchased in 1993. Though my cousin had already accepted a bid from a renter on the property, I was able to convince her to sell it me for the same price after telling her of my plans for a school.

In Haiti, the parties first agree on a price, in this case about $20,000. The seller then presents the current deed to a notary public to perform a title search. Upon finding that good title will pass to the buyer, the notary accepts and holds a deposit from the buyer, then draws up the contract on which the parties will perform at closing. In this case, my cousin and her buyer had only reached the first stage of agreeing on a price. If she had followed through to closing with him, my cousin probably would have had to travel to Haiti to collect payment in cash. In Haiti, most business is done with cash; it is unlikely the original buyer would have thought to wire. As it turned out, I short-circuited the process and spared my cousin the risk and inconvenience of having to travel back from Haiti with a bag stuffed with money. My offer, which she accepted, was payment up front, in full, by wire. I already knew the land and its title history very well because she was my cousin.

So now I had the religious order to run the school, land on which to build it, and through a secondary school friend who was now practicing architecture in New York, a set of drawings for the building itself. Still missing was money for construction, estimated to be $250,000. Another year would pass before I began assembling a list of donors to be solicited. I focused on philanthropic entities that had a track record in Haiti and set about asking each for $10,000 at a time.

Meanwhile, Cardinal Keeler, Bishop Constant, and I were regularly brainstorming about how to accelerate the fundraising. Bishop Constant was familiar with Food for the Poor, an ecumenical Christian organization that had been working in Haiti for a long time. Cardinal Keeler said he knew one of the American Catholic bishops on the board. With these two eminent clerics behind me, the door swung open rather easily when I knocked.

With Bishop Constant accompanying me, I met with the president of Food for the Poor in the latter part of 1998 and asked for a grant of $10,000. The first response was one of distress. The president said he already had so many other projects to support throughout the Caribbean. I made the counter-argument that while his organization was feeding people and keeping them dependent on someone else to be fed, my program was finding a way for people to feed themselves by empowering them with an education. Some two hours later the conversation had shifted from denying a $10,000 request to agreeing to foot the entire cost of construction, along with the services of an architectural firm to supervise it. Rather than draw from the existing grants budget, Food for the Poor would raise money for the school as a separate, discrete project.

As construction began in 2000 and progressed over the course of a year, the cost increased, and I put up an additional $50,000.

I offered to name the school for the president of Food for the Poor, but he declined. I did not want my name on the school either. Too many people and institutions had contributed to this project to name it for any one person. It occurred to me instead to name it for a biblical character who exemplified the life-saving generosity the school would attempt to foster in its students. That character was the Good Samaritan of the Gospels who stopped to aid the man bleeding at the roadside, badly beaten by robbers, and whom several prominent citizens had passed by. The school would serve the poor kids whom people pass by, without even looking at them. For those children, the school would be someone new who comes by, stops, and sees them differently. And so the school opened as Les Bons Samaritains.

Life Changes

As these developments coalesced toward opening the school for the 2001-2002 academic year, I was undergoing three life changes that would launch me fully into this, my next calling.

The first was preparation for my retirement from the Cancer Center at Penn State, effective December 31, 2001, to devote myself full-time to my work in the Church and my mission for Haiti. This departure had been a few years in coming as the new calling sounded louder and louder in my ears.

The next two happened almost simultaneously.

My ordination to the permanent diaconate took place in St. Marc July 5, 2001. A delegation of seventy people flew in from the Archdiocese of Baltimore to be part of it, including Cardinal Keeler and Msgr. Gale-one. Bishop Constant, the principal celebrant for the Mass, ordained me before a crowd of about four thousand at St. Marc's Church in St. Marc. The event was held in this, my original parish church, rather than at the Cathedral of St. Charles Borromeo in Gonaïves, where deacons are otherwise ordained as the step just before priesthood because the Church in Haiti does not have a program for permanent deacons like me. I believe I was the first, and so far the only, permanent deacon ordained in Haiti.

The event held other significance for me as well. As I lay prostrate in front of the altar as the Litany of the Saints was sung for my ordination, I could not help but recall that this was the exact spot, eleven years ago to the day, where my mother's coffin rested during her funeral. The flood of memory became a torrent. It was here, at the funeral, that my family saw me in tears for the only time as I confronted the loss of my mother. It was here that I recalled "Manman Sisi," the nickname by which she was affectionately known to the multitudes who sought her advice—mothers fretting over their teenaged offspring, wives wondering about the fidelity of their husbands, men agonizing over business decisions. It was here that mourners cried out during the funeral Mass "Manman Sisi, wap kite nou!" (Manman Sisi, you are leaving us for good!") The name meant "Mother Sisi," the last word a variation of her Christian name, Lamercie.

After my ordination, outside the church where the customary brass band had once preceded the hearse carrying my mother to the graveyard, I was now driving a car back to the hotel with Bishop Constant, Cardinal Keeler, and Msgr. Galeone as my passengers. A heady discussion ensued as to my next step as an ordained deacon, jolting me from the mournful reminiscence. As I drove, Msgr. Galeone, who had just been appointed to become bishop of the Diocese of St. Augustine, Florida, was proposing me as his successor for the Office of Missions. Cardinal Keeler immediately agreed, pending Bishop Constant's willingness to release me from my incardination in the Diocese of Gonaïves, in which I had just been ordained. Bishop Constant immediately agreed. It proved a most fateful and efficient means of finding my next job as all the parties involved were fortuitously gathered in this small space.

Two days later, Good Samaritans was dedicated. The memories of my mother inundated me again, this time with pride at making this first installment on the promise of giving an education to those who otherwise would have none, like her.

The Estuary

Somehow an unseen hand was guiding this work along a way, with me at the head of the procession. The course it took was more like a meandering river that ultimately finds its embouchure, an estuary. At its destination, the Baltimore/Haiti Project, which I now led as head of the Missions Office of the Archdiocese of Baltimore, would operate at both a local and a regional level.

If anyone has accomplished anything significant for education in Haiti, it is the Church, through its wide-reaching parochial school system. Yet these schools typically educate children through primary school only. Often, the children do not go further because they cannot move from the rural areas to the city for various reasons. Accordingly, at the local level, the plan of the Baltimore/Haiti Project was to strengthen existing Catholic schools throughout the Artibonite river valley. The hope was that some of these schools eventually would become feeders to the James Stine secondary school that opened much later.

As the initiative got underway, some twenty parishes in the Archdiocese of Baltimore were paired with sister parishes in the Diocese of Gonaïves. The paired parishes would pray for each other and exchange visiting delegations. And the Baltimore parishes would raise money through various means, including special collections at Mass, to aid the corresponding Haitian sister. For those Diocese of Gonaïves parishes left unpaired with Baltimore sisters, the archdiocese would send money from time to time to the Gonaïves Diocese bureau of education to distribute among them. The money flowing to the Diocese of Gonaïves, whether from sister parishes or the Archdiocese of Baltimore itself, would be devoted to the following purposes:

➢ First, feeding the children coming to the parochial schools. In many rural schools the children are not sent to school so much to be educated as to be fed. If you do not feed them, they do not come. The expectation would be that students will come to learn and perform at the same level as any well-heeled classmates. But knowing full well that learning does not take place with an empty and aching belly, feeding students during the school day was essential to the plan.

➢ Second, recruiting and keeping devoted teachers, avoiding the high turnover that is rampant among the lower-quality schools. Accordingly, the contributions would ensure that teachers are paid regularly and faithfully, over the course of twelve months. Although the government pays more, it often does so irregularly, so teachers cannot support themselves day to day, keeping them on constant lookout for opportunities elsewhere.

➤ Third, the money would support formation of catechists in Diocese of Gonaïves parishes to send out to the parochial schools, anchoring the religious component of the education there. These catechists also educate a significant group of adults who have grown up identifying as Catholic but without getting around to being baptized.

At the regional level, we applied and amplified these basic principles—feeding students, paying teachers, and improving catechesis—in the overall design of the Good Samaritans program, and later James Stine, drawing students from across the Artibonite river valley. My input in this plan was very direct and personal, along the following lines:

➤ Our student body for Good Samaritans would be drawn from the poorest neighborhoods of greater St. Marc. I believe that raw intelligence and talent are blind to race, sex, and social class but dependent on the environment for realizing their potential. Influencing the environment, as I intended to do at the school, would make all the difference.

➤ There would be no open registration. Students would be handpicked, with a preference for those from the most impoverished circumstances.

➤ Students would enter at the lowest level, at age five for kindergarten, and later at age three after we established the preschool. The idea was to have a group that would come to know each other for twelve or fourteen years, so when one of them becomes president of Haiti, they know whom to call.

➤ The school would admit both boys and girls. Most Catholic schools in Haiti are single-sex, but I wanted young girls and boys to have access to the same education.

➤ We would take only one student per family and attempt to take them in roughly equal distribution from across the various sections of the region.

➤ The students at Good Samaritans would be served a light breakfast and a substantial lunch. The school would not charge tuition but the family would pay for a uniform and for books, at the equivalent of three dollars a year. The point of asking for these small payments was to give the families a stake in the school and its mission.

➤ We would expand the educational program to include music, computers, science labs, English instruction, libraries—things that do not exist in many other primary schools in the country. Because providing all students with musical instruments would be prohibitively expensive, we would instead offer classes in music theory, and a small lab housing a piano and four keyboards. Computer lab training would start in the second grade.

➤ Developing students' analytical skills would be preeminent. Critical thinking is turning out to be the motor for problem-solving, innovative ideas, and inventions. But in deference to Haiti's system of national examination for advancement in education, we would continue to prepare for those tests but supplement the curriculum with exercises to develop thinking for oneself.

➤ The school would be a Catholic school, teaching the faith to all students, though we would welcome students of any religious background. Students who want to convert to the Catholic faith are welcome to do so. As a Catholic deacon, I baptize many of these converts myself. (Impressing this Catholic identity on the school would not be as obvious as it seemed. For various reasons—primarily lack of resources—nearly 20 percent of Catholic schools in Haiti do not prepare children for the sacraments and nearly 40 percent of them do not teach the faith in every grade.)[2]

This would be the foundation for an experiment in education, concentrated in one area of the country, evaluated in five to ten years, improved as needed, and offered as a model to spread to other parts of the country.

---

[2] Final Report of The National Survey of Catholic Schools in Haiti, The Episcopal Commission for Catholic Education, Catholic Relief Services and the University of Notre Dame, June, 2012 (https://ace.nd.edu/files/haiti/Consulting_HaitiForumReport.pdf)

After putting these principles into practice, with some mixed results, we still saw much of the plan fulfilled. Any fellow visionaries attempting to follow this model elsewhere in Haiti—as I fervently hope they do—should plan on one initiative begetting another. For me, this has been a most rewarding aspect of the effort, not unlike the Gospel miracle of the multiplication of the loaves and the fishes.

CHAPTER FIVE
GETTING STARTED

Students bow for the morning prayer with their eyes closed and hands clasped, in silence.

The dedication of Good Samaritans occurred on July 7, 2001, two months after its construction was complete and two days after my ordination. It was an event for the entire city and beyond. Cardinal Keeler presided, joined by dozens of supporters from the Archdiocese of Baltimore and leaders from Food for the Poor. Locally, Bishop Constant was there, along with Haitian priests, students and their families, and the mayor of St. Marc. Several of these guests gave speeches, the point of all of them being that this school would lift up the poor.

Soon after the guests all left, a sadness descended on me. Now I had to prepare the school for opening in September and I did not even know where the uniforms were, much less anything else about how to operate the school. I was wondering what I had gotten myself into. I started praying. Fortunately, a sister from Sisters of St. Joseph de Cluny, who was a native of St. Marc, had taken charge as principal. She knew just what to do.

Finding the Poorest of the Poor

Where do our students come from? A better question might be, given the pervasiveness of poverty in Haiti, how do we find the poorest of the poor? It is an elaborate and somewhat ingenious process. From January to March before the next school year we send recruiters to visit poor sections in St. Marc and surrounding areas. They wander incognito from nine to eleven on weekday mornings, times when schoolchildren are in school. They look for unattended children wearing no shoes, or no clothes at all, or who have reddish hair indicating malnutrition. Sometimes these children are kicking an orange around in an informal game of soccer. These are our candidates, the ones we want.

The recruiters simply approach the child about attending our school and ask where they live. Haitian children, being very respectful of adults, will take the recruiters straight to their homes to meet a parent or guardian. We inquire within as to the age of the child, why the child is not attending school, and the family's economic circumstances. The age of the child is very important so we can have them from age five—later, with the opening of our preschool, age three—onward.

Almost all the adults we speak to welcome the opportunity, though not always for the intended purpose. For those children of suitable age, the recruiters take a photo of one of the parents with the child and leave an appointment card for them to come to the school for admissions screening. On the day of the appointment the principal checks to see that the parent and child who appear at the school match the ones who appear in the photo. We take this precaution because some parents sell the appointment slip to other families for the equivalent of twenty-five or even fifty dollars. Everyone wants to come to this school that gives you nearly everything. The appointment slip is valuable. We have had to turn away a number of parent-child visitors whose appearance did not correspond to the people in the photo our recruiters had taken a few weeks earlier.

At first, we invited about a hundred children, twenty from each of five neighborhoods, to apply for admissions screening in May. From these one hundred candidates for the first class to enter in 2001 we chose sixty-five. Foremost among the selection criteria were, and remain today, which ones seem neediest?

We have since expanded Good Samaritans to accommodate ninety in the class entering in the 2017-18 school year. Total enrollment at the school for that year will be about 500.

Adeline Felisca was the first student we recruited through our methods for the class entering in 2001, though it might be more accurate to say she recruited us. A remarkable girl, she was the one to initiate conversation with the recruiters and ask about an education. Even at that young age, she knew what she needed, though she also needed so much more. When we first saw her at the age of five, she had no clothes on. She was as dirty as dirt. Her mother was dead. Her father, whom she saw rarely, was an alcoholic. She was living temporarily with a friend of the family. We hired a house parent to take her in, apart from her home, together with four other children from situations like that. Adeline reached eleventh grade with us, then transferred to public high school, and so did not graduate from James Stine. Today she is the first from our school to be employed as a teacher at our preschool that opened in 2015.

Another student we recruited early on was living with adoptive parents who had found him as an abandoned infant in a garbage can. We put him with the same adoptive parent caring for Adeline. He did not make it all the way through James Stine, but last I saw him in 2017, he was continuing his education elsewhere with an intention of going into politics. Even for someone who does not graduate from our program, this is precisely the civic-minded ambition we hope to nurture.

Americans learning about the school sometimes wonder about the socialization required for children from such deprived circumstances. Actually, very few of the children accepted into the school are too wild or otherwise unsocialized to be educated. Parents may not know how to read but they discipline their kids in Haiti. Americans who visit cannot believe how well-behaved the children are.

Yet there is no denying that our students inhabit two different worlds, entering one during the school day and leaving it for another when they return home. We see that as a plus. They do not forget where they come from. Some things they are taught at school, such as habits of personal hygiene—washing hands before meals, for example—we hope they will pass along to their siblings and maybe their parents.

Paying the Bills

As implied from our recruitment technique, an inviolable prerequisite for attending Good Samaritans is an inability to pay for all but books and a uniform. Tuition support must come from elsewhere, and it does, mostly from afar. The Mortel Foundation led the initial effort to raise the needed operating costs, though eventually it could not bear the full weight of the school budgets.

Much of the funding now comes from outside sponsors of student scholarships, from people in different parts of the world, including Europe, though mostly in the United States. Some of these benefactors find us through our website and other social media marketing. Many others we draw from the interested people I routinely take with me to Haiti. This is our most effective marketing strategy. If these visitors are sponsors already, they see what their money is supporting. If they are not sponsors, the trip is likely to encourage them to become sponsors. In either case, they return home talking about what they saw, which often produces more sponsors among their friends. As a result, tuition for all students at Good Samaritans is covered either by sponsors or by the foundation. Those students who go on to James Stine are covered, in turn, as to half their tuition either by sponsors or by the foundation.

Anyone wishing to help a student at our schools will learn firsthand that the dollar goes a long way in Haiti. A sponsor can pay $350 to sponsor a Good Samaritans student and $450 to sponsor a James Stine student; in each case the full cost of educating the child for an academic year is covered, except for the costs of books and uniforms borne by the parents. The sponsor commits for one year at a time. Most continue to renew throughout the sponsored child's passage through our schools. It becomes a relationship. In return, the sponsor receives a photo of the sponsored child, the child's year-end report card, Christmas and Easter cards from the child, and various school announcements.

If sponsors make the trip to Haiti to meet the child in person, the friendship deepens. We do try to enforce limits, though. Any additional gifts the sponsor wishes to make, such as presents at Christmastime, we ask be sent to the school for pooling with gifts from other sponsors and the Mortel Foundation. That way, all share in the sponsors' collective generosity and no particular child is favored over others. In turn, we advise sponsors against releasing their addresses to the children or their families lest the sponsors find themselves inundated with requests for more and different kinds of aid than they are prepared to give.

School Days

Good Samaritans and now James Stine as well follow the Haitian Catholic school model for organizing the school day. At seven thirty each morning, the entire school gathers for an assembly that opens with each student bowing in prayer, eyes closed and hands clasped, in silence. After raising the Haitian flag and singing the national anthem, the students again pray, this time aloud, for special intentions, including prayers for their sponsors. The students then disperse to their respective classrooms, where the teaching is preceded by another short prayer and breakfast at their desks. Recess is at 10:00 a.m., and a substantial lunch is served at noon. Class instruction concludes at 1:30 p.m., followed by specialized afternoon activities, including computer lab, science lab, music, and sports.

On Sundays, the students gather again at the school and walk to the parish church, together with two other local schools, for a Mass scheduled specially for schoolchildren.

The liturgical calendar observed by the school is often embellished by various forms of student participation. On the initiative of the students themselves, they established a tradition of each one contributing a few coins each week during the seasons of Advent and Lent. At the end, they use the money to buy food and cook a meal to bring to prisoners behind bars. As our children advance from a state of need to opportunity for a better future, we want them to reach back and help those still in need. You can always give, even from your poverty. That is a vital aspect of the Good Samaritans education. This simple gesture of sacrifice by the students spoke volumes of encouragement for the new educational paradigm.

Another significant celebration of the school year is the feast day of St. Francis Xavier, who was part of the original group of men taking religious vows with St. Ignatius of Loyola, the founder of the Society of Jesus, known as the Jesuits. After missions to several Asian countries, Francis Xavier died of a fever in 1552 while waiting to complete arrangements to extend his mission to mainland China. We typically celebrate the occasion with a Mass, followed by a cultural program of religious skits, music, and poetry put on by the students, and conclude with a reception.

It was the Sisters of St. Joseph de Cluny, not me, who chose Francis Xavier as the patron saint of the school. They said it was because of his life as a missionary and his death in pursuit of that calling. How fitting their decision turned out to be. The December 3 feast day happens to be my birthday. And Francis is also part of my full given name—François Xavier Marie Gerard Rodrigue Mortel. In Haiti, at least in my day, the godfather was the one to name the child at Baptism. My godfather was someone with a reputation for bestowing a string of names. If you look on my birth certificate, that is what you will see, though I long ago dropped all but the name Rodrigue Mortel. The nun who proposed Francis Xavier as the patron saint was not aware of any of this. I thought it was a fantastic coincidence.

Another annual celebration of the school's own devising is Green Day on May 1, coinciding with Haiti's official Labor and Agriculture Day. We turn the national event into a day devoted to the environment. Students exchange fruits and come to school wearing green shirts, ties, dresses, and sometimes elaborate costumes.

This type of symbol is powerful in a country that pays only lip service to preserving the environment while ignoring disaster being done to it. Not far from St. Marc, the city of Gonaïves is a prime example. Situated below sea level, it is only minimally protected by ditches and canals, most of which are poorly maintained. It suffers recurrent floods of run-off mixed with sewage. At our school, students are taught disaster preparedness so that when their turn comes to make policy decisions, they will use a different frame of mind and sound scientific data. Ecology is woven throughout the curriculum.

Like schools all over the country, we celebrate Mardi Gras, in the tradition that my medical school class helped revive in 1959, as I have mentioned. As the celebration has evolved since, primary schools observe it on the Thursday before Ash Wednesday, high schools on Friday, and universities on Saturday, joined by the rest of the country on the Sunday, Monday, and Tuesday before the Lenten austerities begin. Along with most schools throughout Haiti, we devote the entire day to costumed parades, student performances of folkloric and religious music and dances, and skits—all presided over by a "king" and a "queen" of the Mardi Gras elected from among the students.

I Am Lifted Up

Of course, we celebrate our own school history as well. The fifteenth anniversary of the founding of Good Samaritans was a milestone for us, and for me especially as a founder. From the beginning, I have traveled from my home in Hershey every two or three months for visits to the school of at least a week to ten days. Mostly, I just check on the mundane tasks of running a school. Each time I come, though, there are reunions with students. They all know me and greet me as I come in the door. But for the fifteenth anniversary of the founding of Good Samaritans, they honored me in a way I will never forget.

The celebration that day began with a parade through town. Cindy Goldsworthy, a teacher from Pennsylvania making her second trip to St. Marc for the occasion, gave the best description of it in her blog:

> The touches I will always remember. The small hands that grasped mine as we marched and sang through the streets of St. Marc in a celebratory parade, the handshakes of the parents who expressed their gratitude to us during the celebration, the taps on the arm to get my attention from the many children who simply wanted to connect with us in some way remain in my heart.
>
> So what did I experience? I experienced overwhelming feelings of goodness. Goodness that comes from people wanting to help other people; goodness in the innocent faces of children who are grateful for what is being done for them, and goodness in the hearts and minds of both Haitians and Americans who share this world and hope for a better future for all children.

As the procession ended back at the school, several of the students lifted me and carried me aloft. Willis Gunther, a visitor from the Cathedral of Mary Our Queen in Baltimore, remembered it vividly for our school website: "When the Haitian national anthem concluded, the children swarmed Dr. Mortel and literally swallowed him up. He disappeared in a sea of uniforms only to be raised up and carried, as if he were a feather, all around the school courtyard."

Singing the Story

Sometime in the third year of operation of Good Samaritans, a small group of the original teachers offered to compose music and lyrics for a school anthem. It would take the form of a hymn. The result was an allegorical tale of the Good Samaritan of the Gospels doing his work in Haiti. Since its wholehearted adoption by the school, the hymn has become the accompaniment to all school events. Students and staff sing it with a fervor that heartens me, gives me goose bumps, each time I hear them.

Below I provide my own English translation from the original French of our hymn, followed by the French for those who might appreciate the richness of the original.

"GO, AND DO THE SAME"

1. In Jericho one day
   On the winding road
   Leading to Jerusalem
   A sick, deprived and lonely man
   Needed to be cared for.
   Many were those who saw him
   And did absolutely nothing
   But a caring and compassionate
   Good Samaritan stopped and assisted him.

Refrain:
   Let's be always among those
   Who express love not only in words
   But also in action.

2. In Haiti, as it is all over,
   Numerous are children
   Living in abject poverty,
   Deprived of both food and education.
   People have seen them
   And just walked by
   But a caring and compassionate
   Good Samaritan took steps
   And provided assistance.

   Refrain

3. Good Samaritan, thank you
   For dedicating both your fortune and love
   To the improvement of mankind
   You, who care for the wounds of all neighbors,
   Especially the wounded children
   Abandoned on the road
   May God bless you in return.

   Refrain

4. You, children of the Good Samaritan
   You will travel a road
   Where poor, ill, and lonely people
   Will be waiting for help.
   Be sensitive to the needs of others.
   Be the helping hand.
   Love God, love your neighbor.
   Love yourself.
   We are all brothers and sisters.

   Refrain

And here is the hymn in the original, as our students sing it.

"VAS, ET TOI FAIS DE MÊME"

1. A Jéricho un jour sur le chemin
   Sinueux qui descend de Jérusalem,
   Dépouillé, souffrant, un homme à lui même,
   Délaissé avait besoin bien de soin.
   Nombreux étaient tous ceux
   Qui le virent ainsi par terre et ils
   L'abandonnèrent, mais tout ému
   Le Bon Samaritain, de compassion lui
   apportait soutien

Refrain:
   Soyons toujours de ceux-là qui aiment
   Non pas de paroles mais d'actions

2. En Haïti, et partout sur la terre, voila
   Tous ces enfants dans l'affliction
   Laissés sur le chemin de la misère,
   Privés et du pain et de l'instruction.
   Les ayant vus, nombreux ont passé outre.
   Les abandonnant ainsi sur la route,
   Mais tout ému le Bon Samaritain,
   De compassion, leur apporte soutien

Refrain

3. Merci frères du Bon Samaritain, qui
   Dévoue dans l'intérêt des humains,
   Votre argent ainsi que votre amour.
   Que notre Dieu vous bénisse en retour.
   Vous qui bandez les plaies
   Et les blessures, portant les fauchés

Sur votre monture, lors du voyage
A chercher vos prochains,
Enfants blessés, laissés sur le chemin.

Refrain

4. A vous enfants du Bon Samaritain,
Lors de votre long voyage en chemin,
Que de souffrants seront délaissés
Par terre, attendant un appui salutaire.
Soyez dévoués dans l'intérêt des autres,
Dans la vie d'une manière ou d'une autre.
Comme vous-mêmes aimez Vos Prochains
Nous sommes tous frères, faisons le bien.

Refrain

St. Marc is a city on Haiti's west coast, part of the Artibonite Department (each of Haiti's ten provinces is known as a department). As it is throughout the country, poverty is rampant and many make a modest living by selling items in the market.

The dedication of Les Bons Samaritains (Good Samaritans) occurred July 7, 2001. Cardinal William H. Keeler, archbishop of Baltimore, presided, joined by dozens of supporters from the Archdiocese of Baltimore and leaders from Food for the Poor. Locally, Bishop Emmanuel Constant of Gonaïves attended, along with Haitian priests, students and their families.

For the Good Samaritans inaugural class, we invited about a hundred children, twenty from each of five neighborhoods, to apply for admissions screening in May 2001. From these one hundred candidates, we chose sixty-five. Students receive breakfast and lunch daily and receive annual medical and dental care from American volunteers.

Good Samaritans is run by qualified teachers and staff. The school is the #1 private employer in the city and employees are paid all twelve months of the year.

Top: Good Samaritans support staff

Middle: Good Samaritans teachers and administrators

Bottom: Good Samaritans teacher in class

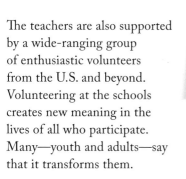

The teachers are also supported by a wide-ranging group of enthusiastic volunteers from the U.S. and beyond. Volunteering at the schools creates new meaning in the lives of all who participate. Many—youth and adults—say that it transforms them.

The need for a secondary school was obvious. The new school, named for its main benefactor, Collège James M. Stine (James Stine College) would stand on three of the ten acres Mortel had purchased in 1993. The site was not suitable for Good Samaritans because the neighborhood was too inaccessible to the poor and very young children we were seeking. It would now be accessible to such children as they grew older. Construction began in January 2010, the same month as the devastating earthquake in Port-au-Prince.

Above, Cardinal Edwin F. O'Brien, Dr. Mortel and his wife, Cecile,
after the dedication ceremony of James Stine College in 2012.

Scenes from the dedication ceremony:
below left, James Stine College student choir sings;
below right, Cardinal O'Brien

Many people from Haiti are not really proud of where they are from. Our students come to us with that attitude. But we teach a different outlook, starting with my experience as someone who is unabashed about the poverty he came from and who has accomplished quite a lot.

When students reach their final year at James Stine, we ask them to write short biographies of their time there and at Good Samaritans. The theme that I find running through all these student reflections is that they are no longer embarrassed about their origins, and now are confident of where they are heading.

James Stine students at the school library.

The need for early childhood education was evident as our students progressed through high school. Our preschool opened in 2015 for 200 three- and four-year olds. The school building was dedicated in January 2018 by Bishop Ronald Gainer from the Diocese of Harrisburg. The celebration included a group of board members and supporters from the U.S. as well as my sister, Dinah. Students and faculty celebrated with song and dance.

The Notre Dame de Lamercie literacy school originally opened to teach parents of the Good Samaritans students in 2002. It now serves nearly 100 adults and teaches basic literacy and arithmetic in a four-year cycle within the Good Samaritans school building.

I've always enjoyed time spent with the students at our schools; it has become a real family. We always try to provide these children with affection and time to play, as well as quality role models, not knowing what their home life may look like.

I'm inspired to see that some of our graduates and "Good Samaritans alumni" are already giving back to their communities. They have had supply drives to support victims of Hurricane Matthew and have also run a program to bring Christmas gifts to children in poor neighborhoods. These young adults are our mission in action.

CHAPTER SIX
COME AND SEE

Students of Good Samaritans with young American visitors.

Our school is run by qualified paid staff. They are paid less than their peers in public schools, but they are paid regularly throughout the year, which is part of the attraction for them. Beyond that, they are supported more than most of their professional peers by a wide-ranging group of enthusiastic volunteers from Haiti and far beyond. Volunteering at the schools creates new meaning in the lives of all who participate. Many say it transforms them.

Our parents form the first line of unpaid help at the school. They provide security for the children as they enter and leave the building. Because there are motorcycles racing everywhere in town—many as part of an informal fleet of taxis—the parents encircle an area around the gate to prevent the motorcycles from penetrating. They make sure each student is picked up by a parent or other authorized person. During parades, which are frequent, the parents also maintain discipline and watch over the spectating children. Crowd control is never a problem; the parents handle all of it.

Finding Direction

Other volunteers follow a pattern that started with my trip to Albert Schweitzer Hospital in the 1970s, and that has replicated itself in countless trips since. American friends, colleagues, and acquaintances come to me with curiosity about Haiti. Or they hear about what I am doing in Haiti and wonder how I do it without any government help. I invite them to come with me on one of my regular visits to see for themselves. Almost invariably, they fall in love with the country and return home with a lifelong yearning to contribute to the work.

While staying with us, the visiting volunteers give precious gifts of their time, their enthusiasm, and themselves. As I mentioned, some of these visitors decided to sponsor students. Sometimes these visits also result in major gifts. One example is Jeff Remington, a middle school science teacher in Palmyra, Pennsylvania, near Hershey, who visited Good Samaritans and James Stine and loved what he saw. An outstanding teacher, Jeff later won national recognition for his work and donated his prize money, about $15,000, to build a science lab at Good Samaritans. With the new lab came a continuing relationship. Now bright students from Palmyra Area Middle School and Good Samaritans share the same schedule of science experiments and exchange their respective observations and results via the Internet.

Other visitors have discerned their life direction from the experience. Rachel Bowles, originally from Ellicott City, Maryland, participated in one of the Archdiocese of Baltimore's first mission trips to visit Good Samaritans in 2003. Haiti "got under my skin," she later explained. Indeed, after going on to college, where she majored in French, she joined the Peace Corps to work in a Francophone country in Africa. After that, and after completing graduate study in international relations, she came to work at the Mortel Foundation. By 2017 she had taken over as director of operations for High Hopes for Haiti, which is essentially the successor to the Mortel Foundation as chief fundraiser and funding source for the schools.

The Doctors

Among our visitors are doctors who have committed to returning twice a year to provide preventative medical care as an added feature of our program. Working from a room set aside at Good Samaritans to house donated chairs and other equipment, three dentists from the Archdiocese of Baltimore come for a week in the fall and spring to treat students who need dental work. One of them had started out trying to set up a clinic at a rural parish that had been paired with his parish in Maryland, as part of the Baltimore/Haiti Project. But the remoteness of the location and the lack of electricity to power his instruments made practice there too difficult. Setting up a permanent dental suite at Good Samaritans offered a far better alternative.

He and his colleagues were soon joined by two optometrists from the Diocese of Harrisburg who check students with vision problems. As of the end of 2017, we were in discussion with a pediatrician to make similar visits.

These children would never, ever receive such care otherwise. Growing up, I did not see a dentist until I was in medical school, and only then because the dental school was located conveniently next door. These services for students are available to our faculty as well, which offers a further advantage in recruiting teachers. Medical plans are virtually unknown in Haiti. Everything is cash. If you go to the hospital, you have to buy your own syringes and fluids, for example. There is no public health care, which is why many of the NGOs operating in Haiti dedicate themselves to that.

The Children

What seems to touch the volunteers—both young and old—most deeply during these visits is the conduct of our students. They see the children playing in the school courtyard in the morning, then lining up immediately in straight lines for prayer when the bell rings. In the classroom, as soon as a visitor appears at the door, the students stand up and do not sit back down until the visitor invites them to do so. During recess, they approach and talk. They are just friendly kids. All these little things impress the people who come to the school. The discipline really catches their attention. They do not see that kind of thing in the United States.

One such visitor, Pat Brady, head of the Religion Department at Archbishop Spalding High School in Severn, Maryland, has led groups to volunteer in St. Marc since 2002. Considering why he had just completed another trip—his sixteenth—he wrote: "I realized that my answer is a very selfish one. I go because I want to be with the kids. As soon as I walk through the gates of the Samaritan school, I am greeted by energetic (usually sweaty) kids that have huge smiles on their faces and seem to be genuinely happy to see me. Despite the language barrier, they have no problem at all communicating their affection and trust in me."

The Rev. Brian Wayne, Catholic chaplain at Millersville University of Pennsylvania, came with me on his first trip to Haiti and returned twice in later years leading college groups. As happened with Pat Brady and others, he was drawn by the children. Overcome at first by the poverty, especially by "seeing the children hungry around town," Father Wayne saw hope in how the people—especially the children—handled their deprived circumstances.

"You realize that what shocks your sensibilities is their ordinary, and in the midst of their ordinary, they choose to be joyful and hospitable," he wrote in an email to the Mortel Foundation. "What touched me most was that so many of these kids dream of making Haiti even better. They are faith-filled kids, enriched by a desire to help their fellow Haitians. I think that is the foremost goal of these schools.... They realize that is why they have been gifted [with] this education and it is a joy to see them hope for such great things. I look forward to seeing the way in which these schools affect Haiti for the good in the many years ahead!"

Giving, Receiving Even More

Thanks to my continuing connections with the Diocese of Harrisburg, where I live, and the Archdiocese of Baltimore, where I work, the supply of volunteers is further supplemented by young people—like those led year after year by Pat Brady and others—who take weeklong mission trips during their summer break to staff summer sessions at Good Samaritans and James Stine. They spend their time with us teaching conversational English (beyond the basic grammar structure that our faculty is able to provide), arts and crafts, science experiments, and sports. In return, we take them on field trips, often to rural Haitian parishes, and otherwise immerse them in Haitian culture.

Most come from around the Archdiocese of Baltimore and the Diocese of Harrisburg, and some from even farther afield. Bishop Alemany High School in Los Angeles, for example, comes during the school year, during the week of Ash Wednesday. In the mind of their faculty leader, previous mission trips to other countries had too closely resembled vacations. Looking for something more substantial and mission-oriented, the school found us on the Internet. They keep coming back. As Don Levan, director of campus ministry there, explained it, his students feel they are witnessing, perhaps participating in, social transformation. "These schools are so important to the people of Haiti whose poverty extends beyond material wealth to a dearth of social services and opportunity," he said. "Education provides them with a chance to see themselves and their country in a different way while it empowers them to create a better future."

Most of these visiting volunteers from America return home thinking they gained even more than they gave. After their mission trip in 2017, the students from Archbishop Spalding High contributed their impressions to our school website. The excerpts below give a sense of what they found in St. Marc, and what they brought back with them.

Every single day he came in with a smile on his face and not once did he ask any of us for anything. I have never met a more genuine person. One time I told him I liked his necklace and so he asked me if he could give it to me. I said no and that all I wanted from him was his time and his friendship. I was blown away that a kid who has less than half of what I have would offer to give me something of his. That was [a] time when I really saw God in him.

— Carly O'Brien, on her encounters with a James Stine student.

This trip has encompassed a lot of firsts: first time I've ever showered in the rain, first time I've ever traveled without family, first time I've dripped in sweat for seven days straight, first time I've truly felt a language barrier, and the first time I've 100% known that I want to give up my life to serve others.

— Audrey Donahower

Before Haiti, I was unhappy with my life. My family got on my nerves, I took my home for granted and, most importantly, I took God's love for me for granted. After my Dad's death in 2009, my relationship with God came to a halt.... I blamed Him when times got rough and did not trust Him. Being surrounded by kids who are so full of life and love made me realize that God is in everyone and He will be with you to help you through every obstacle.

—Torrie Bordes

[A]s Americans we live in our own little world and push the unacceptable things out of our mind.... While most citizens of Haiti do not have a lot of money, they have the most important things: love, hope, and laughter. They show love in their daily lives and their actions, they hope for the future, and laugh to bring joy to each other's lives.... No, the Spalding crew can't make extensive changes for the people of Haiti, or simply St. Marc, in just a week. However, we can take what lessons we learned and what we learned about the students of St. Marc and spread them to the rest of the world. Okay, the world is a big idea, we'll start with the Spalding community.

— Sydney Madden

All I could see for miles was dirt and mountains. Seeing the environmental disaster that Haiti has become made me feel a sadness I have never felt before. However, the week I spent with the teens from the Stine school gave me a joy I've never experienced in my life.

— Chris Comer

I came to this trip already wanting more, and now that our time in Haiti is over this feeling is overwhelming. To live with a purpose beyond personal luxury, and make a meaningful contribution in the lives of others. One day I hope to return with much more than a suitcase and a smile.

— Trinity Walker

CHAPTER SEVEN
THE EARTH MOVES

*Rodrigue Mortel sits with a child
living in a refugee camp.*

Good Samaritans was well advanced in its mission, and plans to add a secondary school were underway when, on the afternoon of January 12, 2010, Haiti suffered an actual earth-shattering experience. Shortly after school had let out for the day, the ground began to shake, with a force measuring 7.0 on the Richter Scale, which means major damage anywhere it occurs—and worse in a place like Haiti. The epicenter was about fifteen miles southwest of Port-au-Prince, but the shock reverberated through much of the country, including St. Marc.

Leveling in Port-au-Prince

Densely populated greater Port-au-Prince was hit hard. Initial reports said three-quarters of its buildings had toppled. Vulnerability to the violent shaking had been exacerbated by lax enforcement of building codes, inferior construction materials, and inadequate seismic proportioning in design. The simple economic fact of construction in Haiti is that cement is expensive. If builders can get away with it—as they did more often than not—they built with less cement between the blocks in a simple cinderblock structure than the building code formulas required.

The devastation ranged from countless flattened homes to severe damage to the buildings of national significance. The National Palace, which serves as the official residence of Haiti's president and houses its parliament, was damaged beyond repair and had to be demolished two years later, though there are plans to rebuild. Nearby, the city's Cathédrale Notre-Dame de L'Assomption lay in near ruin, its roof collapsed. Among other buildings broken open were prisons. Crime was rampant in the aftermath.

By official government estimate, the quake left 316,000 dead, among them about forty thousand schoolchildren and one thousand teachers. That amounts to just over 3 percent of the total population, making this earthquake the deadliest in terms of share of population killed. More than 300,000 homes throughout Haiti were destroyed or critically damaged, resulting in the displacement of more than a million people. Some 60 percent of the national administrative and economic infrastructure was lost, 80 percent of the schools, more than 50 percent of the hospitals, and more than 180 government buildings were destroyed or damaged.[1]

---

[1] Overview of the 2010 Haiti Earthquake, by Reginald DesRoches, M.EERI; Mary Comerio; Marc Eberhard, M.EERI; Walter Mooney, M.EERI; and Glen J. Rix, M.EERI; U.S. Geological Service. (https://escweb.wr.usgs.gov/share/mooney/142.pdf); and Final Report of The National Survey of Catholic Schools in Haiti, The Episcopal Commission for Catholic Education, Catholic Relief Services and the University of Notre Dame, June, 2012 (https://ace.nd.edu/files/haiti/Consulting_HaitiForumReport.pdf)

Whom Shall I Send?

I was in the United States at the time but joined a Catholic Relief Services (CRS) medical mission to my homeland as soon as I could, leaving on twenty-four hours notice from Miami, all against the advice of family and friends. I traveled light, bringing just two pairs of pants, some T-shirts, protein bars, and a sleeping bag.

The next morning my team arrived to an aftershock almost as bad as the first blow, measuring 6.4 on the Richter scale. We set up our surgical and medical care quarters in the courtyard of a Catholic hospital in Port-au-Prince that had crumbled, burying alive some eighty patients and visitors. I sprinkled holy water on the rubble that covered them and treated survivors, many of whom had lost family and homes. Most needed treatment for more than their physical injuries. It was not unusual to complete treatment and tell a patient he could go home, only to hear that he no longer had a place to call home.

During my second week in post-quake Haiti, CRS moved our team to an outpatient clinic for its employees and their families. Of those I met, most had lost a spouse or a child. Nearly a hundred children came to me with minimal physical injuries but major emotional ones. Despite having no formal training in psychology, I was able to draw upon thirty-five years experience helping patients through the trauma of cancer. I knew how to listen, which was the best I could do for many of these traumatized people.

I left Haiti February 2 and returned to my parish in Hershey especially prepared for the homily I was scheduled to give three days later on Isaiah 6:3-8, at the end of which the prophet hears the voice of the Lord saying, "Whom shall I send? Who will go for us?" Indeed the Lord sends all of us in one way or another. I have been fortunate to hear my own calling with particular clarity.

Displaced

Though fifty-five miles from the epicenter, St. Marc was not spared. Buildings around the city, including many schools, were destroyed. And all schools, regardless of the damage, were closed until the risk of students returning was assessed by government engineers. By all outward appearances, Good Samaritans was unharmed, but inspectors discovered a crack running through the ceiling of several of the ground floor rooms. We had enough money in the operating budget to complete the repairs; the problem was the time it took.

The students did not come back to class until April. We posted the notice of closure, as we do with all other important announcements, on large blackboards on the school's front gates. The posting, spread from there by word-of-mouth from the people who read it, is the only way we can inform parents and the larger school community in any uniform way. Very few have access to telephones or email. Often, it takes about two weeks for the word to reach everyone.

Meanwhile, St. Marc was inundated with displaced persons. Many families who had moved to Port-au-Prince years ago renewed their family connections and returned to St. Marc, abandoning their flattened homes in the capital. Local school authorities sought to place their children in new schools. At Good Samaritans we took sixty children from displaced families. A few returned to Port-au-Prince after a few years, but most stayed. Working from the theory that there is always a place for somebody else, we accommodated them, and the school just got bigger.

Once the fissure in the school ceilings was repaired and school was authorized by the government to reopen, we posted announcements to that effect on the school gate blackboards. As the word slowly spread, students trickled back to class. But we faced a further challenge of convincing many parents and students alike that it was safe to do so. The displaced families from Port-au-Prince, where the destruction was much worse, remained terrified. And their fears rubbed off on our pre-earthquake constituency as well. Many were traumatized by the loss of more than three hundred thousand of their fellow citizens in the quake. Eventually, for the stragglers, we made use of volunteer psychologists provided by the local school district to counsel individual students in overcoming their fears of stepping back to the classroom.

Not only was the program at Good Samaritans disrupted, so were the cost and schedule for completing the James Stine building. In the latter case, the result was ultimately for the better. The foundation for James Stine had just been laid when the quake struck. It did no damage, but we had to change the building plans to meet new building code provisions and stricter enforcement of existing ones. The biggest alteration was to turn the initial plan for a continuous C-shaped structure into three separate but joined wings. That way, any future earthquake destruction to any one of the wings would be less likely to force a domino effect of further destruction on the others.

Nevertheless, it took some effort to convince the religious order with which we had contracted to provide teachers and administrators for James Stine that they would be safe in a multistory building. When their national headquarters in Port-au-Prince collapsed in the quake, many of the personnel working on the second floor survived. But all of those on the ground floor, including some of their seminarians, were crushed to death. The order wanted us to provide a single-story residence at James Stine. Only through much review of the new building codes addressing earthquake safety did we persuade them to occupy the third floor, which is the top floor, of the building that would rise as home to the new school.

CHAPTER EIGHT
WIDENING THE CIRCLE

Rodrigue Mortel in front of James Stine College.

Even before we began planning to build upon the success of Good Samaritans with other new schools, an opportunity to expand Good Samaritans presented itself unbidden in the form of a phone call from a stranger. It was an attorney representing the estate of a Maryland man who apparently had read about Good Samaritans and wanted to benefit the school after his death. The attorney said the family was quarreling over the estate and that I should just accept the money without making contact to thank them or learn more about our benefactor. The bequest was for $250,000, from out of the blue! We had to start thinking about what to do with it.

Only when the money came did we see the need. Good Samaritans was built as twelve classrooms, and one office spread across just two stories. There was no storage space and no offices for staff beyond the main one for the principal and her secretary. The gift was more than enough to finance a third story, which was completed in 2005. With the new space, we were able to add offices, storage, and guest quarters consisting of bedrooms on the third floor and a kitchen and dining room on the second.

Meanwhile, our academic needs were outgrowing Good Samaritans even with a third story added. As our first class at Good Samaritans approached sixth grade, the school's highest grade, we decided we could not let them disperse to an uncertain future. Otherwise, many might have ended their education right there. We did not want to lose them. So we added a seventh grade, then an eighth and a ninth grade. In doing so, however, we found that the teachers hired for these new grades fell short of our standard. They were not nearly as proficient as those teaching grades one through six. The proof lay in the results of the ninth grade national exam of 2011. Most of our students had to stay back a year. The problem was that fewer truly qualified teachers were available to teach at these higher grades. Moreover, the Good Samaritans principal, who excelled at leading a school for grades one through six, was less competent in evaluating candidates to teach beyond those grades.

It was time to take the education experiment to another level.

James Stine College

The need for a secondary school was obvious. The path to staffing and funding it was not. From experience, I knew where to start. I approached my two bishop friends.

Our first stop was the Christian Brothers, whose reputation for running schools in Haiti remained as high as it had been in my day. With Bishop Constant at my side during the appointment, I asked them about taking charge of this new secondary school venture, just as the Sisters of St. Joseph de Cluny were doing at Good Samaritans. Despite their reputation, however, the Christian Brothers said their vocations had declined to the point of having to vacate some of the government-owned schools they had operated, including L'Ecole Frère Herve, where my own education began in St. Marc. They referred us to another religious order, Les Clercs de St. Viateur (Clerics of St. Viator) and opened the door for us there. Also known as the Viatorians, this order of priests and brothers has a wide-ranging apostolate in education that involves many lay associate members. It takes its name from a fourth-century catechist at the cathedral in Lyons, France. In short order, the Viatorians agreed to take on this new school.

For funding, Cardinal Keeler sent me to the James M. and Margaret V. Stine Foundation, which had benefited church projects before.

James Stine had been the founder and CEO of the Cressona Aluminum Company, now part of Alcoa. I knew of him from Penn State where his company was a major employer in the region. He had been a great benefactor to the university even though he was actually an alumnus of the University of Maryland. Shortly before James Stine's death in 1997, he and his wife had moved to Maryland, where they continued to contribute to cancer research at Johns Hopkins University, other hospital- and church-related programs through their foundation.

His widow, Margaret Stine, received Cardinal Keeler and me at her home in Annapolis. By that time, Good Samaritans was winning good notices at home and abroad as the new way forward for Haiti, all as I had hoped. On the strength of this, I presented her with an estimate of $2.5 million to build the school. She offered that her foundation might give half a million. I did not respond at all, letting that figure hang in the air. Out of the long pause, she responded again, doubling the grant to one million. I proposed naming the school for her late husband; she said that would be nice. With that commitment in hand, I was able to spread the word among other donors to gather the rest, from the Archdiocese of

Baltimore, the Mortel Family Foundation and others.

The school would stand on three of the ten acres I had purchased in 1993 for $25,000, far below market price, from a former teacher who had heard from a mutual friend of my aspirations to start a school. Though the site had not been suitable for Good Samaritans because the neighborhood was too inaccessible to the poor, very young children we were seeking, it would be accessible to such children as they grew older and could manage public transportation. Also, this new school would accept additional students from very different, upper-middle- and upper-class backgrounds.

The main reason for widening the franchise of the secondary school was the difficulty of extending the Good Samaritans model of free tuition to this more sophisticated, and expensive, level of education. We would charge tuition to those who could afford it and who could pass a demanding entrance exam. Graduates of Good Samaritans would be admitted automatically and with a scholarship covering half the tuition. Of course, paying the remaining half would still pose a sacrifice for these poor families. In practice, though, most of our Good Samaritans families are able to make the transition. Some have relatives working abroad who are willing to chip in toward the tuition. Others work extra jobs. These families respond much as my mother did to my schooling opportunities. They would do anything to educate their children, particularly at a secondary school reputed to be the best in the region.

The new school, named for its main benefactor, opened as Collège James M. Stine (James Stine College) in 2011, encompassing the grades seven through nine we had initially tacked onto Good Samaritans and taking those students, along with several newly admitted ones, the rest of the way through their secondary education. Cardinal Edwin F. O'Brien, who had succeeded Cardinal Keeler as archbishop of Baltimore, dedicated a new building that consisted of twenty classrooms, plus living quarters for the Viatorians, all surrounded by athletic fields.

Major gifts to the school did not stop with the opening. Three years later, in 2014, Dr. and Mrs. Steve Lucking from Hershey donated a fully equipped science lab. As with so many other guests visiting the school, Steve Lucking, a pediatrician I knew professionally, had expressed an interest in my work in Haiti. He had accompanied me to the dedication of James Stine College, liked what he saw, and acted on it. (He is also preparing to make a further gift—of his professional time—as the pediatrician who will join the dentists and optometrists in their semi-annual medical missions to the schools.)

James Stine has grown from an initial student body of 210 to 585 as of the end of 2017. Its governing board comprises two members from the Mortel Family Foundation, two from the Clerics of St. Viator, and one chosen by the bishop of the Diocese of Gonaïves.

The school operates on principles of meritocracy, yet we do all we can to prevent anyone from falling by the wayside. The performance of the students, drawn from the full spectrum of social and economic classes, cuts across this divide. But for those poorer students who do struggle to keep up, the Mortel Family Foundation employs one of the teachers to monitor their academic work and to provide remediation and help with study skills as needed. The effort brings most lagging students up to par, which is essential if they are to fulfill the school's goal of creating new, better-educated citizens. There is no such aid, however, for the purely aptitude-based selection of students for varsity athletics, school band, and other extracurricular programs. As with the academics, participation in these activities ranges across the socio-economic array.

In a relatively short time, James Stine has made a sweeping difference in the educational performance of its students. A few statistics tell the story. In the academic year 2016-17, a total of 11,856 students spread among 312 schools in the Artibonite Department took the national secondary examination. In 63 of those schools, none of the 513 students attending them passed. In 52 schools in the department, encompassing 1,854 students, the pass rate was 20 percent or less. At James Stine, where 42 of its students took the exam, the pass rate was 100 percent.[1]

The students sitting for the national secondary school exam actually are divided into three different study tracks: liberal arts, math, and science. Each year the government recognizes the top ten scores in these areas among students in each of the nation's departments. In Artibonite, one James Stine student was recognized in each of the math and science tracks, and in the liberal arts track, all ten of those recognized were James Stine students.[2]

Failure can force drastic change as its remedy. Sometimes success brings change as well, in order to create more of it. The latter is what occurred after the Sisters of St. Joseph de Cluny announced their intention to leave Good Samaritans at the end of the 2016-17 academic year. They explained their departure in terms of a need to shift precious personnel to another school they were running in St. Marc. It was a primary school to which they were adding a secondary school. Fortunately, because of our new relationship with the Viatorians, a replacement stood ready in the wings. He was a young Viatorian brother teaching at one of the order's other secondary schools. After deciding against taking final vows of lifelong commitment to the order, he accepted appointment as the new principal of Good Samaritans, starting in the fall of 2017.

Patricia Chairs Preschool

Having extended the education project to secondary school and preparation for university, I turned next to stretching it again in the other direction, to the earliest years. We noticed the original group of sixty-five Good Samaritans students falling behind long before their number had dwindled to four by graduation day in 2015. Among the James Stine students, those who had entered school earliest tended to do better. It became overwhelmingly apparent that we needed to start earlier in ed-

---

[1] Ministère de l'Education Nationale et de la Formation Profesionnelle 2016/2017, Bureau National de Examens d'Etat, Direction Départmentale de l'Artibonite
[2] Ibid.

ucating the poorest of the poor. Numerous studies have found that, especially among poor children, early education makes a huge difference.

Finding the solution and the means to pay for it took longer. Once the Mortel Family Foundation board voted in 2014 to form a preschool, we acted with dispatch. We leased space nearby, within an existing school for *restaveks*, to take three- and four-year-olds, starting in September of 2015. Like Good Samaritans, the preschool is tuition-free. The students eat breakfast and a substantial lunch there, and receive annual preventative medical, dental, and eye care check-ups. Our recruitment of three-year-old candidates for the preschool follows the same strategy as previously for the five-year-olds for Good Samaritans—incognito visits to poor neighborhoods during school hours to search for unsupervised children. Yes, children as young as three play in the streets all over some parts of Haiti.

This was a temporary step. The seed funding for a permanent building came, again, from a benefactor with a history of supporting church-related projects. This time it was Samuel Chairs Jr., founder of a family-owned construction company in Ellicott City, Maryland. The Haiti connection had come through his parish, Our Lady of Perpetual Help, also in Ellicott City. The pastor, who was looking to form a sister-parish connection in the Diocese of Gonaïves under the Baltimore/Haiti Project, went with me on a visit to the schools in St. Marc. Returning with love for the country running through his heart, the pastor passed along his impressions to his parishioner, Mr. Chairs, who had previously established an endowment with the Catholic Community Foundation to support education in Haiti. Mr. Chairs responded with a further gift toward the building, asking that we name it for his late wife, Patricia Chairs, who had a special love for young children.

The Chairs family, the Mortel Foundation, and the Archdiocese of Baltimore each contributed one-third of the total construction cost of $300,000. The preschool moved into its new building in September of 2017, and the dedication of it, by Bishop Ronald W. Gainer of the Diocese of Harrisburg, was set for January of 2018. The building sits at the opposite end of the same downtown block occupied by Good Samaritans. Nestled between the two schools are three private residences and the pied-a-terre I maintain for my visits to Haiti.

In the meantime, in the years before opening James Stine and the preschool, I undertook two other initiatives in education, one more successful than the other.

Notre Dame de Lamercie

Education must be holistic, reaching even beyond the child's growth of mind, body, and spirit. We wanted to influence the home environment by including their parents. As a tribute to my mother whose name was Lamercie, and as a gesture to help many parents still in her predicament, we opened the Notre Dame de Lamercie (Our Lady of Mercy) adult literacy program at the school in 2002. My mother used to practice a special devotion to Our Lady of Mercy, making an annual pilgrimage to a Notre Dame de Lamercie parish outside St. Marc on the September 24 feast day.

Admission to the program is open but with priority for Good Samaritans parents who might one day want to read and write enough to help their children with homework. Classes run four afternoons each week, beginning at the end of the children's school day. Teaching proceeds in Creole at first, then transitions to French in the second year onward. No tuition is charged. At first, the enrollment in each class of thirty adults was split about evenly between men and women, but in more recent years became predominantly female. Despite our efforts at scheduling for convenience, attendance can be difficult for a parent weighed down with household chores and the care of young children. High turnover of adult students threatened the program after we lost our first director and the support of a Canadian charity that had subsidized it.

In 2016, however, the Mortel Foundation took over the funding, hired a new director with expertise in adult education, and lengthened the course from four years to five. The program quickly revived. We also plan to add craftwork classes for adults interested in learning to make crafts for sale in Haiti and abroad. This last feature should succeed where earlier, unrelated efforts to provide cooking and sewing classes did not. The sewing class in particular fell victim to the lack of employment opportunities. Seamstresses already struggle to compete in a low-end clothing market glutted with street vendors hawking second-hand clothes donated from the United States.

The classrooms once used for cooking and sewing instruction were converted to guest quarters for our many visitors. This renovated section of the school can accommodate as many as fifteen people in guest rooms and a private dining room.

Centre Cardinal Keeler Ecole Technique de Bigot

There is a trade school in Gonaïves named for Cardinal Keeler, the Centre Cardinal Keeler Ecole Technique de Bigot (Cardinal Keeler Center) but it is now completely separated from any of my education efforts, even though I was the one to push hard for major funding of it from the Archdiocese of Baltimore.

The idea for a trade school originated with Bishop Constant whose strenuous efforts to raise money for one in his diocese had brought only a single grant of about $20,000 from a French charity. He next appealed to Cardinal Keeler, but Cardinal Keeler favored funding programs over new brick and mortar. However, the Archdiocese of Baltimore had recently sold some of its real estate for a significant sum. Later, I successfully appealed to the archbishop to set aside 10 percent of the proceeds for the Baltimore/Haiti Project. Under this arrangement, the project, which was part of the Office of Missions I had been appointed to lead in 2001, would have discretion to devote a portion of that money toward building the trade school. In the end, nearly all of it went to construction at a cost of $800,000, all as a gift to the Diocese of Gonaïves.

Following Bishop Constant's plan, the priests of the Society of St. Francis de Sales (a Catholic religious order known as the Salesians), who specialize in vocational education, would run the program. The money received early on from the French charity would fund construction of a residence for them there.

In 2003, Bishop Constant had to step down, having reached the mandatory retirement age of seventy-five. His successor, Bishop Yves-Marie Péan, was less interested in close management of the project and let the Salesians have free reign. Eventually, the Salesians asked the Archdiocese of Baltimore for another $50,000 to purchase equipment for the school. It was granted. But another request for support in 2007 was turned down as it became apparent that the school had deviated significantly from Bishop Constant's vision after he had put the Salesians in charge.

The original plan was for the school to teach four basic trades— plumbing, electrical, woodworking, and metallic construction. The school would recruit twenty students to study each trade, half from Gonaïves and half from St. Marc. Instead, the Salesians introduced other trades and recruited no one from St. Marc. The order took it over as a purely Salesian mission, which was not Bishop Constant's intent. Despite major support from the Archdiocese of Baltimore in the past, the Salesians refused to admit any archdiocesan representation on the school's board of trustees.

Still, the archdiocese did not give up. Cardinal O'Brien, who by then had succeeded Cardinal Keeler, paid a visit to the trade school during his trip to Haiti to dedicate James Stine College in 2011. He promised the Salesians in the administration there that he would recommend continued support to his incoming successor, Archbishop William Lori, on the condition that the school provide financial records for the previous two years. As the head of the Missions Office, I followed up with a call to the school and was told there never had been a formal budget; they just ran it day to day. Even now, I know very little of what goes on at the trade school despite my role with the Archdiocese of Baltimore in helping to bring it about. For that reason, I continue to count this institution as one of the five I founded in my educational experiment for Haiti.

I plan to try again, this time by building a trade school somewhere on the seven acres that remain of the ten I purchased back in 1993. As of late 2017, we had the concept; we had the land. We just needed a benefactor to fund a building and teachers to instruct in the various trades. From experience, I have every confidence that we will find the support.

Buildings as Brand

There are now five Mortel Foundation-supported schools housed in four buildings. We built them, each in its own style, each for its distinctive purpose. Yet they are united in one aspect of their appearance. Each building is cream-colored, with brown trim, and over the front door of each is a large bay window divided by white vertical grillwork. The name of the school is emblazoned across the top of the grill in large brown letters. Whatever the layout of the rest of the school, whether an existing one or another to be built in the future, this bold grillwork with the sign on top will be our brand.

The look positions each school as facing the future. The new, educated generation of Haitians is stepping forward from the doors beneath.

Even Higher Hopes

Eventually, our mission outgrew our financing structure, which depended largely on the Mortel Foundation passing the proceeds of its fundraising to the schools. As a private family foundation, the Mortel Foundation is required to distribute a minimum of 5 percent of its asset value each year. Because of the high value of the school land held by the Mortel Foundation, this meant distribution of more than our schools' operating budgets could absorb. This was a wonderful problem to have, but a problem nevertheless. We addressed it by engaging a lawyer in 2015 to help set up a new, public charitable organization, High Hopes for Haiti. As required under IRS rules, I had to review thousands of names of persons and organizations on a government list of possible terrorists to ensure that the money flowing out of the United States to Haiti under this new organization would not finance any hostile groups. After that, IRS approval was relatively swift, coming in 2016.

The main advantage of this new arrangement is that High Hopes for Haiti can absorb all of the required distributions from the Mortel Foundation and receive further gifts from other charitable organizations and institutions, which my family foundation could not do. The foundation will continue to own the land occupied by the schools. I am currently looking into other purposes for it, including micro-financing of small businesses in Haiti. Meanwhile, High Hopes for Haiti has become the public face of fundraising and promotion for the schools.

CHAPTER NINE
FINDING THEIR PLACES

Graduates of James Stine College

In general, people from Haiti do not like to tell anyone where they are from, especially if they are from poor rural areas. Many will just say they are from Port-au-Prince. They are not really proud of where they are from. Our students come to us with that attitude. But we teach a different outlook, starting with my own experience as someone who is unabashed about the poverty from which he came and who has accomplished quite a lot. When students reach their final year at James Stine, we ask them to write short biographies of their time there and at Good Samaritans.

What they have to say about themselves on the cusp of graduation from secondary school, after so many years with us, is one of the most valuable measures of the success of the educational mission.

What follows are excerpts from a sampling of recent graduates. The year of graduation is indicated next to the student's name, with a line about where their studies have taken them as of the end of 2017. These reflections (as I have translated them from the French) bring out many of the themes discussed so far: the invitation at age five from the streets to the school, appreciation of a hot lunch at school, awareness of the support for their education by people they have not met, and aspirations toward a future they could not have imagined before. Students are candid about their struggles with poverty, with the academic challenge, and with the inevitable conflicts arising from encounters with wealthy students—typically for the first time in their lives—upon entering James Stine. The theme that I find running through all these student reflections is that they are no longer embarrassed about their origins, and now are confident of where they are heading.

Student Voices

Johnson Cirius, class of 2015, is studying English in the United States in preparation to apply for acceptance to an American university.

I am the son of a market woman and a teacher. Growing up, my modest childhood always served as a source of motivation and determination. Miserable lodging, hunger, loneliness, and many other setbacks combined to make life difficult.

The troubles of my life led me to the Good Samaritans school whose mission is to serve the poor—the economically, socially, and intellectually deprived children.

Shy and timid in my adolescence, I didn't have many friends, but those I had were the best. Words fail me in explaining the happiness these friends brought me, whether they were Haitians or Americans.

My time at the Good Samaritans school was spent striving daily to live up to its reputation as a Good Samaritan, sometimes leaving behind friends who meant the world to me. When I advanced to James Stine College, I had to get used to school without some of my good friends, but I made new friends with whom I got along as well. As the years passed at James Stine, I made great memories despite life's difficulties. Within all my dreams and ambitions, I strive constantly to be a Good Samaritan like Dr. Mortel, [Bishop] Constant and many other generous people like the Sisters of St. Joseph de Cluny, the Clerics of St. Viateur as well as all of the teachers who worked with me from kindergarten through high school.

Josue Jean François, class of 2015, attends medical school in Port-au-Prince.

I am the oldest child in my family, and since I was a baby, I caused my parents much worry. When I was five years old, I had the chance to be admitted to the Good Samaritans school, and that was the beginning of my favorite part of my life. I made new friends and followed the instructions given by the teachers. It was the start of my love of learning. In pursuing my studies, I paid nearly nothing thanks to donors who supported my studies with the help of the Mortel Foundation, to whom I owe so much.

At the beginning, the fact that someone was financially supporting my studies didn't have much effect on me, but as I got older, I realized that these supporters—even if I didn't know who they were—were like parents to me, and I took that to heart.

I want to become a doctor—a great doctor—and use my position to help the weakest like many have done for me.

My message is this: give in return for all that you have received.

Roselanda Therzy, class of 2015, teaches at the Patricia Chairs Preschool.

I come from a family where daily life was a struggle. My mother's name is Mirlande and my father, who is deceased, was named Rosemond. I have two sisters, Rose-Vasty and Guetie. It was my mother who worked in the market to try to afford school for me and my sisters. During the early years of school-

ing, I encountered a lot of difficulty—nights without sleep to study and work. I suffered much during these years but resigned myself to study and work without eating when my mother couldn't afford to feed us. Thanks to Dr. Mortel who founded the Good Samaritans school, my mother's burdens were eased. When I was at the Good Samaritans school, the food and education I received allowed my mother to use what little money she made to help my sisters eat and go to school since she didn't always have enough money to support us all every day. I was very lucky when I went to school. I spent ten great years at the Good Samaritans school and I am so proud now to say that I am an alumna of this school.

After ten years at the Good Samaritans school, I attended James Stine College, and I had difficulty fitting in with my new classmates. It took months for me to adapt. At the beginning there were even students who didn't want to befriend students from the Good Samaritans school, saying that it was a school for the poor and that we weren't smart. But we showed them that we were also intelligent as we worked hard to succeed. Despite what some said during that first year at James Stine College, I was never discouraged because I knew what I wanted. I could only attend James Stine College as a former Good Samaritans student because my mother could never afford to send me there.

Cedner Honorable, class of 2015, aspires to become a physician.

I am the son of a tailor and a farmer. Growing up in St. Marc, at age five, I began kindergarten at the Good Samaritans school where the costs of schooling were paid for by foreign supporters. This school was my destiny since my parents didn't have enough money to pay for my education.

Shy but well-behaved, I completed all of my primary education there, working hard and making friends with my classmates and with Americans who visited.

When I finished at Good Samaritans school, I had to leave many friends behind as I continued my studies at James Stine College. It was at James Stine College where I learned to overcome my shyness.... Now, I want to study medicine and become a doctor like Dr. Mortel and like other members of the foundation. I want to become a Good Samaritan to help others in need.

Loveson Ainé, class of 2017, is studying at university in Haiti.

I am one of twelve children in my family. My mother worked in the market and my father is a farmer. I was raised in St. Marc by one of my older sisters. When I was five years old, I was given the opportunity to attend the Good Samaritans school where I completed my primary education. Then I continued my studies at James Stine from 2011 to 2017.

During my fourteen years of classical studies, I was supported by a sponsorship program of the Mortel Foundation. Because of this, I took my education very seriously in order to succeed academically. I always worked hard to achieve my goals, and I have always wanted to continue my studies abroad to make a name for myself.

Nesly Sterling, class of 2017, is waiting to hear about acceptance to university in Haiti for the 2018-19 academic year.

I came from a poor family as the sixth of seven children. In 2001 I was orphaned, as my mother passed away. That same year I enrolled into the Good Samaritans school, a school that welcomed the poor and destitute.

I suffered a difficult childhood. My first day of school, I didn't have my mother to comfort and support me, so one of my aunts stood in her place. I was looking forward to school, but once I got there, I sobbed because for the first time I was away from home and surrounded by strangers. Little by little, I adjusted and found myself in a real school family where I was surrounded by brothers and sisters like me. This became a real turning point in my life.

From 2001 to 2011, I spent ten years in this school. These were the best ten years of my life. Then in October of 2011, I transferred to James Stine College to continue my secondary studies. I spent six years there, five of which were the most difficult of my life as I encountered different types of people—wealthy children whose parents were political leaders, policemen, and many others—who mocked me.

In July 2017 I completed my classical studies in hopes of embarking on further studies or a new professional journey. This is my dream, but my family cannot afford to support these next steps. No matter where I go, I am proud to say that I am an alumnus of the Good Samaritans school....

Acerneau Aurelus, class of 2017, works part-time for Good Samaritans while preparing to study computer science with a specialized program in St. Marc.

> I am twenty years old and come from a poor family where I'm the oldest. My mother was the sole provider for our family as a housekeeper.

> I remember well when I was of school age, but because of financial reasons I was not in school. I was playing in the street and suddenly some adults caught up with me and took my photo. From this day on was the beginning of a new me, like a newborn child. This was an opportunity that the Mortel Foundation gave me. I began school and was given all the necessary school supplies. We were given breakfast each morning and a hot meal for lunch. To be poor and attend this school opened my mind and gave me everything. I went through all of my primary studies at Good Samaritans school and then my secondary studies at James Stine College, with hopes of continuing on to university with the support of the foundation. I want to study computer science. Thanks to the knowledge I gained at the Good Samaritans school, I've been able to start my first business (Young Aurelus) where I do digital paintings and graphic design.... I will work every day for a happy life so that my children don't have to go through what I've gone through. I want to invest my time in helping the weakest in my town and in my whole country in the same way that I was helped.

Adeline Felisca, originally part of the class of 2017, but who finished secondary school elsewhere, came back to teach in the Patricia Chairs Preschool.

> *My mother, Erana, died when I was two, and my father was an alcoholic.*

> *From 1996 to 2002, I lived in a very poor area of town. I didn't attend school, but God sent me a Good Samaritan, named Dr. Mortel, who gave me the opportunity to attend his school, the Good Samaritans school. I love this school where I completed my primary education.*

> *If I continue my studies, it's thanks to Dr. Mortel and his beautiful school along with all the teachers that helped me. I was the first student enrolled in the Good Samaritans school by Mrs. Lafortune and Mrs. Dinah. I toy with the idea of one day having a school of my own that welcomes needy children.*

A Grateful Parent

Parents, too, join their children in taking pride in their circumstances and in what their children have achieved. The strongest witness to this is their service as volunteers assisting in many of our school functions. One of them, Mrs. Leonce Joseph, whose daughter Emula was a student in Good Samaritans at the time, spoke most movingly about this at the fifteenth anniversary celebration at the school. Here is some of what she said:

> *Except for family, school is the oldest institution, the social group the most indispensable to mankind. It is the epicenter*

of education and the extension of the family unit. In other words, school is a mandatory step in life.

Indeed, the literacy level of a nation is an indication of that nation's values. Consequently, as parents, we claim that, likewise, a society is as good as the value it gives to education....

Dr. Rodrigue Mortel, the founder, the man with the vision, we have not found words strong enough to thank you and express our gratitude. But in his infinite love, the Lord will save a special place for you in his kingdom. You have achieved what no one before you could accomplish in this city.... But thanks to your dynamism and your administrative ability, our school has become what it is today, a school of reference where the fundamental right to education and health care as well as the need to feed the children are respected and carried out. In our school nothing is missing.

Whether we are hearing from the student or the parent, we find people motivated by gratitude, accomplishment, and a strong sense of a role in a society that once seemed to have no place for them. This is the new generation that is finding its place, preparing to lead Haiti.

CHAPTER TEN
PERSONAL INFLUENCES

Cardinal William Keeler and Rodrigue Mortel during the dedication of the Cardinal Keeler Center.

The two incidents I have described as turning points toward my experiment in education—the eviction from my childhood home and my visit to the Albert Schweitzer Hospital—were just catalysts. I want to conclude by delving into the formative influences that caused me to react as I did to those events and to follow up on them with action.

Life-long Faith

My Catholic faith has defined me from the earliest of times; my mother saw to that by her word and example. As a youngster, I was fascinated by her ascetic practices of fervent prayer and fasting. After Sunday Mass she often stayed on for a good hour, kneeling before the tabernacle of the Blessed Sacrament and saying her rosary, almost falling into a trance. This vivid image of my mother casting her fate into the hands of God deeply affected me. I have tried to do the same.

My own serious practice of the faith began as an altar boy, at age nine, learning all the rituals, which were conducted in Latin in those days. Fortunately, I was an early riser. The daily Mass was at 5:30 a.m. and the first of several Masses on Sunday started at 4:00 a.m. That Sunday Mass was always packed. Some of the parishioners were coming directly from parties spilling over from Saturday night.

Before each Mass, I assisted the priest in donning his vestments in the sacristy. I handed him the alb to put over the cassock, the cincture to fasten the alb, the stole to hang around his neck, and the chasuble to drape over everything. It fell to me to know which occasions called for the priest to wear a cope, or a benediction veil, or a surplice. As Mass began with a procession, I would swing the heavy censor to keep the incense smoldering inside and the perfumed smoke wafting through the church. The hymns, the chants, the a cappella performance by the cantor all moved me. So too did the homily. Visiting priests who were great preachers attracted crowds, their words lingering as a topic of conversation around town for the week to come.

Going to Sunday Mass was as natural as breathing; it was ingrained in the culture. Certain feast days such as Corpus Christi in June still turn out crowds across the country. The procession behind the consecrated host can stretch for miles, stopping at different houses festooned with flowers for the occasion. What Haiti may lack in financial assets it more than makes up in cultural and spiritual riches.

I worked not just on Sundays but at daily Masses and special occasions. It was a coveted role for which the pastor selected just a few boys each year from a large and eager group. One reason for the fierce competition was that the parish paid me the equivalent of sixty cents a month for my services, plus a little more for weddings and funerals. Most of my pay was deducted and applied to purchasing schoolbooks. This amounted to a bonus for families like mine. Serving the altar also stirred aspirations in me to the priestly vocation, with all the gravitas that came with it. Though I eventually turned my fascination briefly to flying airplanes, then to practicing medicine, the attraction to liturgy never went away. My ordination to the permanent diaconate in 2001 eventually fulfilled a part of those early longings.

My duties as a deacon today straddle boundaries of Pennsylvania and Maryland and the seas and cultural differences separating the United States and Haiti. In the Diocese of Harrisburg, where I have special episcopal permission to function, I am assigned to the parish of St. Joan of Arc in Hershey. There, I preside at baptisms, weddings, and funerals, and deliver the occasional homily at Mass. In Baltimore, where I act under further episcopal permission, I have no connection to any specific parish but continue my work with the Office of Missions as a part-time consultant. In Haiti, where I am officially incardinated, my responsibilities reach further to meet the exigencies there.

During my visits to St. Marc, priest friends sometimes invite me to travel outside the city to rural parish centers that serve as many as a dozen remote village missions accessible only on foot or on motorbike. Catechists conduct religious education courses for adults in these villages. The classes may meet in a small building or under a big tree. When they are ready for baptism, the catechumens come to the parish center, sometimes more than a hundred at time, to receive the sacrament. The reason for so many baptisms of adults is that when a child is born in a poor rural area, survival, more than baptism, is the preoccupation. Many people are Catholic more by default than by conviction. They may not know what Catholic is; they just know they are not Protestant. Eventually, when such an adult wants to learn more, he enters a catechism class that lasts two years.

The mission of the diaconate is to render service. As a deacon, I feel better equipped to help people in need, as Jesus commanded, and with him always at the center of these endeavors, whether in the form of feeding the hungry or baptizing them. To me this is sublime. It is a way to touch the lives of others. But I firmly believe that the best way to help others is to help them reach a position where they can help themselves. The results last longer.

Strong Women

Alongside, and not behind, every successful man stands a strong woman. I am a living proof of that. Strong women have helped and guided me at every turn and continue to surround me, especially in my family.

Of course, the first such woman was my exceptional mother. She made all the difference. With her in my life, growing up poor was a blessing; it trained me to survive and thrive even in adversity. Poverty never defined me; my character did, and still does. Though now inhabiting the opposite end of the financial spectrum from where I started, I still hold the same values and do not regard myself as being a better man now, living in First World comfort, than when I was struggling in the Third World. Traveling the road of poverty and meeting affluence along the way, I know that personal failure can be associated with both. My story, as I would have it told, is that this boy born from a great mom learned early on that self-respect, through hard work and honesty, begets the respect of others. Most of all, this boy found out while growing up that the give and take in life means giving as much as receiving.

Another strong woman in my life was my sister Dinah who dropped out of school so that the family could afford to send me to complete my secondary education at a better school in Port-au-Prince. When the time had come for me to continue my schooling beyond high school, my mom had to make a choice. My sister, four years my senior, was studying in

Port-au-Prince at a trade school for culinary arts and sewing. She was lodging at the house of a friend of the family that had previously allowed us to remain in their house after the eviction. Unable to pay for both of us to stay with this family, my mom asked Dinah to return home so I could go to the big city to finish my schooling. My sister never resented it. She is one of the few people I trust wholeheartedly. We have remained close from the time we were little.

Finally, my wife Cecile is my ideal companion and biggest cheerleader. We married in 1971, a year after the end of my first marriage, which had fallen apart over geographic separation in my pursuit of professional opportunity as well as a cultural separation owing to differences in Haitian versus African-American ways.

I could not have sustained my string of successes without Cecile, who embraced her role of wife, friend, and mother, while sometimes doubling as father during the frequent absences demanded by my career. I consider myself a family man who does not put work ahead of family. As part of that role, as head of the household, I believe it is also important to provide for the family and to do whatever that may require so long as it takes the form of honest work. It is not an either/or proposition; rather, work and family represent two sides of the same coin.

Since I had to travel so much, Cecile acted as travel agent for all the arrangements. Over time, she succeeded so well at these tasks, picking just the right combination of airline, hotel, and sights to see, that by the time of my retirement in 2001, I had accumulated more than 1.5 million travel miles with American Airlines Advantage.

Most of all, her patience never flagged. My wife was always the first to explain to my children the reason for my absences, the first to cheer them up about major moves—once in 1978 to Paris for my study at the University of Paris, and again in 1989 to Washington, D.C., while I served for a year as a congressional aide. She was instrumental in fostering an atmosphere of harmony in our blended family of two children from my previous marriage and the two we had together.

Enduring Habits

Throughout my professional life, I have wanted others to see the potential of the poorest children in Haiti, just as I saw the potential in my own children who grew up in far more comfortable circumstances in America. Nurturing this potential involves seeing something in a child that he may not yet see himself. That is how it was for me growing up poor in St. Marc and ascending to achievement and recognition that I could not have imagined. As one who has lived this transformation and sought to encourage others to bring it about for themselves through education, I can almost say that talent and money are the least of it. Character counts most of all. If you develop character, the success and the money come eventually.

As I told the James Stine students in the commencement speech in 2015, the character traits of honesty, integrity, productivity, assiduity, and determination are essential to true success in life. Here is how I expressed those traits in practical terms for the students that day, and as I would explain my experience with character formation on any other occasion as well, the lesson being the same for everyone:

Honesty. Do not say yes when you want to say no. Do not say no when you can say yes to something that is truly within your power and would benefit others if you were to do it.

Integrity. No one is perfect; we know that. You will make mistakes but when you do, never shift the blame. Own up to it, take full responsibility, move ahead, and try not to repeat the same mistake.

Productivity. When you accept a job or a position of responsibility of any kind, make sure you know what is expected of you. Then give it your all. People can tell when you do. Just as important, people can also tell when you do not.

Assiduity. Part of working hard involves paying close attention to every detail. This includes details of your own personal presentation, of which punctuality is very important. Avoid tardiness like a plague if you want people to rely on you.

Determination. Where others see obstacles, you should see opportunity. When you get knocked down, get right back up, and resume course. Success depends on finding opportunity, not clinging to security.

These are the habits that first brought me to the attention of Bishop Keeler in Harrisburg and that backed up my proposal to the president of Food for the Poor, and so much more. Professionally, these habits also brought me to the attention of three physicians who were instrumental in the shape and progress of my medical career. Put another way, these habits of character, developed as they were in schools of academics and of hard knocks, brought me to where I am today.

Nowadays my thoughts turn toward making sure my works survive me. The next generation is already laying the groundwork. The first recruited student has now become a teacher in the preschool. Down the road, I would like more teachers to come from among our alumni who have faced the same hardships that future students will go through. I also hope that some of the future graduates will turn out to be great scientists, humanitarians, but most of all that they also take every opportunity to help others.

I feel blessed. I have accomplished feats beyond my dreams. If I were to write my own epitaph, it would go something like this:

> The road I have traveled is called education. It has been long and difficult at times, but my companions made the trip possible. First is my faith in God, source of my strength and hope. My next is my mother, who made every imaginable sacrifice to allow her children to have a better life. In turn, my sister never ceased to cheer from the sideline. It culminates with my wife, Cecile, far more than my better half, who helped me to climb whenever the road led up a mountain. Lastly, my children, source of joy and happiness, always ready to celebrate with us when we reached the top of every mountain.
>
> The trip has not ended. Although the seeds we planted have begun to germinate, the tree we may never see. It has been enough for me to plant and see the sprouts breaking through the hard ground.

ABOUT THE AUTHOR

In telling the story of his efforts to promote education as the solution for Haiti and its people, Dr. Mortel has alluded only glancingly to the medical career that came before. An earlier book, *I Am From Haiti*, by Rodrigue Mortel, M.D., as told to Judith T. Witmer, Ed.D., recounts that part of the Rodrigue Mortel story in great detail. For purposes of this book, the summary below is offered to complete the profile of this man of many parts.

Early practice

Upon graduation from medical school in 1960, Dr. Mortel served his required government service practicing general medicine for two years in rural parts of the country, first in St. Michele de l'Attalaye, to the north and inland from St. Marc, then in the larger town of Arcahaie, closer to Port-au-Prince.

He left his homeland in 1962 for graduate study at Hôpital de la Misericorde in Montreal, Quebec, Canada. A year later, he made his move to the United States, first to Philadelphia to train in obstetrics and gynecology at Mercy-Douglass Hospital and later at the Hahnemann Medical College and Hospital, then to New York to specialize on gynecologic oncology at Sloan Kettering Cancer Center.

Academic Career

Dr. Mortel joined the faculty of the Penn State College of Medicine as an assistant professor in 1972, advancing to full professor in 1977, chairman of the Department of Obstetrics and Gynecology in 1983, and to associate dean and founding director of the Penn State University Cancer Center in 1995.

Scientific and Policymaking Work

Much of Dr. Mortel's scientific research at Penn State and elsewhere has been devoted to new ways of treating women with endometrial cancer, a form of cancer that begins in the uterus. His interest in this area developed over a sabbatical at a cancer research laboratory at the University of Paris in 1978, which led to appointment as a fellow of the Ligue Nationale Française Contre le Cancer and as a professeur a la Fondation de France.

In 1988, Dr. Mortel was selected by the Institute of Medicine of the National Academy of Sciences as one of six Robert Wood Johnson Health Policy Fellows. This prompted forays into policymaking, notably as a health aide for a year to Rep. Sander Levin, a Michigan Democrat who was then chairman of the Health Subcommittee of the House Ways and Means Committee. He also served on the advisory board of the National Cancer Institute from 1979 to 2000. As a member of the Society of Gynecologic Oncologists, he monitored applicable legislative issues and led the effort to establish a gynecologic oncology section within the National Cancer Institute.

In related work, Dr. Mortel created and became chairman of the Gynecologic Cancer Foundation, served as president of the American Society of Gynecologic Oncologists in 1994, chaired the education committee of the International Gynecologic Cancer Society, and acted as an examiner for the American Board of Obstetrics and Gynecology and the Australian Board of Gynecologic Oncology.

Religious Vocation

The story of Dr. Mortel's calling to the deaconate of the Catholic Church is told in the book, along with the assignments that came with it through both the Archdiocese of Baltimore and the Diocese of Harrisburg. In addition, he was appointed to the Commission on Social Doctrine for Harrisburg and to the board of directors of the Weston Jesuit School of Theology in Boston.

Honors

Dr. Mortel's work has been recognized in many significant ways by an array of institutions. Among the first of these acknowledgements was the the United States Public Health Service award in 1970. Among the most cherished was the Horatio Alger Award in 1985.

His fellow ex-pats recognized him through the National Organization for the Advancement of Haitians, which honored him with its Award for Excellence in Education and Health in 1997, and the Haitian Institute in Montreal, which conferred its award for outstanding achievement in medical education and research in 1999.

Penn State has recognized Dr. Mortel in many ways, both during and after his career there; specifically with: the Faculty Scholar Medal in 1986, for outstanding achievement in health sciences; the Doctors Kienle Center for Humanistic Medicine Award in 2002, for demonstrating the highest standards in dealing with patients, colleagues and community; the naming of one of its four learning societies, established in 2013, as the Mortel society; the Penn State Honorary Alumni Award in 2015; and election as president of the Penn State College of Medicine Emeritus Faculty Organization in 2017.

As a gesture of thanks for these honors, Dr. Mortel and wife endowed two visiting scholar lectures at the university, one in the Department of Obstetrics and Gynecology and the other at the Cancer Center.

For the practical aspects of his practice, Dr. Mortel was recognized in 1993 and 1997 as one of the Best 401 Doctors for Women in the United States.

Publications and Public Appearances

In addition to *I Am From Haiti* mentioned above, Dr. Mortel co-authored with Jean de Brux and Jean Pierre Gautray *The Endometrium: Hormonal Impacts* (Plenum Press, New York, 1981), dealing with the physiology and physiopathology of the menstrual cycle. He has contributed chapters to other books and written 135 articles for various periodicals, including opinion pieces for the *New York Times* and the *Washington Post*.

In further pursuit of his interest in inspiring young people, Dr. Mortel has given numerous motivational talks at high schools and commencement speeches at colleges. He has also taken to the national stage with two appearances on Robert Schuller's television program, "Hour of Power."

Family

Dr. Mortel is the father of four children. From his first marriage came Ronald, now a statistician in the field of environmental science; and Michelle, now a nurse who married and gave birth to grandchildren Brenda and Trevor. With his wife, Cecile, he has two more daughters: Denise, who has three children, Jonathan, Kayla and Alyssa; and Renée who has two children, Alexis and Brooklyn. Denise has an MBA but currently stays home to care for the children. Renée is an assistant state's attorney in Prince George's County, Maryland.

SPECIAL THANKS

So many people have helped me in making my life as rewarding as it has been, enabling me to try to return the favor by helping others. Although that gratitude surely has found its expression in parts of the story I tell in this book, I must single out three physicians I worked with early in my career and a fourth who inspired me to write. To them I extend a particular gratitude here.

Dr. Helen O. Dickens was head of the obstetrics-gynecology department at Mercy-Douglass Hospital in West Philadelphia, where I served an internship in 1963. Telling me my talent and potential exceeded what the hospital could offer, she arranged an interview for me at the Hahnemann Medical College and Hospital.

The interview was a success. Dr. George C. Lewis, chairman of the obstetrics-gynecology department at the Hahnemann offered me a prestigious residency slot. But I had to be quite frank in telling him I could not take it at the stipend offered. The amount was substantially lower than what I was making at Mercy-Douglass. My financial needs were greater, too because my mother had just suffered a stroke. Dr. Lewis thanked me for my candor and advised coming back when I was ready. With that assurance of future advancement, I was able to continue for another year at Mercy-Douglass receiving compensation sufficient to bring my mother and my sister to live with me in hospital quarters. With the extra money I was also able to help my mother build a house of her own when she recovered her health and returned to Haiti.

By 1965, I was ready to revisit the offer from Dr. Lewis at the

Hahnemann and begin a wonderful journey in the field of obstetrics and gynecology. He was the one who pointed me toward academic medicine. And it was he who introduced me to Dr. John L. Lewis (no relation) at Memorial Sloan Kettering Center in New York and provided a glowing letter of recommendation as I applied. There was just one position available at the time at Sloan-Kettering—the very best in the field—and I got it.

These three physicians encouraged me and guided me to where I ended up, in a niche occupied by very few people but one from which I could help many.

A fourth person, Dr. Reynald Altema, is a practicing physician and writer, but most of all a friend whose example and gentle urging led me to start writing about my vision for education in Haiti.